RICHARD II

RICHARD II

William Shakespeare

WORDSWORTH CLASSICS

This edition published 1993 by
Wordsworth Editions Limited
8B East Street, Ware, Hertfordshire SG12 9HJ

ISBN 1 85326 042 8

Printed in England by Clays Ltd, St Ives plc

INTRODUCTION

SHAKESPEARE WROTE two great historical tetralogies on the subject of kingship. Of the two, the one sometimes known as *The Wars of the Roses*, comprising *Henry VI Parts I, II and III* and *Richard III* covering the years 1422-1485 was the first to be written and performed. The other, comprising *Richard II, Henry IV Parts I and II and Henry V* was written later, although it covers the period from 1377-1415.

Richard II opens with the quarrel between Thomas Mowbray, Duke of Norfolk, and Henry Bolingbroke, Duke of Hereford who is the son of the king's uncle, John of Gaunt, and therefore cousin to Richard. Richard resolves the dispute by disallowing trial by combat, and quite arbitrarily exiles the antagonists. John of Gaunt is the one counsellor who can sway the influence of the callow king, but he dies, broken-hearted, after delivering one of Shakespeare's most moving speeches 'This royal throne of kings, this scept'rd isle'. After his death, Richard confiscates his estates to pay for his Irish wars. When Bolingbroke hears of this, he returns from exile determined to reclaim what is rightfully his, but the very act of doing so constitutes rebellion. He takes the great castle of Berkeley, and when the king's Welsh supporters join him, Richard has no choice but to surrender to Bolingbroke. The king is sent to London, where he abdicates in favour of Bolingbroke, who styles himself Henry IV, but does so in such a way that all are aware of the coercion, which casts a great shadow of doubt over the legitimacy of Henry's kingship. After an assassination attempt on Henry is foiled, Richard is sent to Pomfret Castle, where he is murdered, thereby confirming the illegality of Henry's actions.

The theme of kingship is one that fascinated Shakespeare. Its burdens, rewards and risks are dealt with variously from the arch-villainy of Richard III and King John to the hero King Henry V. That the political content of the plays was considered dangerous in the volatile politics of Elizabethan England is demonstrable by the fact that the deposition scene was omitted from the printed texts until after the death of Elizabeth I, and it is thought that the Earl of Essex paid for a performance of the play the day before his abortive revolt against the queen.

Richard II was first performed in 1595, and while the main source is Holinshed's *Chronicle*, it owes much to Marlowe's *Edward II;* Shakespeare's Richard is a finer achievement than Marlowe's Edward, though the part is not strongly or even variously supported. In fact, *Richard II* is more of a lyrical monologue than any other play by Shakespeare, and the monologues are superbly written.

Details of William Shakespeare's early life are scanty. He was the son of a prosperous merchant of Stratford upon Avon, and tradition has it that he was born on 23rd April 1564; records show that he was baptized three days later. It is likely that he attended the local Grammar School, but he had no university education. Of his early career there is no record, though John Aubrey states that he was a country schoolmaster. How he became involved with the stage is equally uncertain, but he was sufficiently established as a playwright by 1592 to be criticized in print. He was a leading member of the Lord Chamberlain's Company, which became the King's Men on the accession of James I in 1603. Shakespeare married Anne Hathaway in 1582, by whom he had two daughters and a son, Hamnet, who died in 1586. Towards the end of his life he loosened his ties with London, and retired to New Place, his substantial property in Stratford which he had bought in 1597. He died on 23rd April 1616 aged 52, and is buried in Holy Trinity Church, Stratford.

Further reading:

E Kantorowicz: A Study in Medieval Political Theology 1957
R B Pierce: Shakespeare's History Plays: The Family and the State 1971
M M Reese: The Cease of Majesty 1961
E Tillyard: Shakespeare's History Plays 1944, 1962

RICHARD II

The scene: England and Wales

CHARACTERS IN THE PLAY

KING RICHARD THE SECOND

JOHN OF GAUNT, *Duke of Lancaster* } *uncles to the*
EDMUND, *Duke of York* } *king*

HENRY BOLINGBROKE, *Duke of Hereford, son to John of Gaunt; afterwards King* HENRY IV

DUKE OF AUMERLE, *son to the Duke of York*

THOMAS MOWBRAY, *Duke of Norfolk*

DUKE OF SURREY

EARL OF SALISBURY

LORD BERKELEY

BUSHY }
BAGOT } *servants to King Richard*
GREEN }

EARL OF NORTHUMBERLAND

HENRY PERCY, *his son*

LORD ROSS

LORD WILLOUGHBY

LORD FITZWATER

BISHOP OF CARLISLE

ABBOT OF WESTMINSTER

SIR STEPHEN SCROOP

SIR PIERCE OF EXTON

Lord Marshal

Captain of a band of Welshmen

QUEEN *to King Richard*

DUCHESS OF YORK

DUCHESS OF GLOUCESTER

Lady attending on the Queen

Lords, Heralds, Officers, Soldiers, two Gardeners, Keeper, Messenger, Groom, and other Attendants

KING RICHARD II

[I. I.] *A great scaffold within the castle at Windsor, with seats thereon, and a space of ground before it*

'*Enter* KING RICHARD, JOHN OF GAUNT, *with the* DUKE OF SURREY, *other nobles and attendants.*' *They ascend the scaffold and sit in their places, the King in a chair of justice in the midst*

  K. Richard. Old John of Gaunt, time-
      honoured Lancaster,
Hast thou according to thy oath and band
Brought hither Henry Hereford thy bold son,
Here to make good the boist'rous late appeal,
Which then our leisure would not let us hear,
Against the Duke of Norfolk, Thomas Mowbray?
  Gaunt. I have, my liege.
  K. Richard. Tell me, moreover, hast thou sounded him,
If he appeal the duke on ancient malice,
Or worthily as a good subject should   10
On some known ground of treachery in him?
  Gaunt. As near as I could sift him on that argument,
On some apparent danger seen in him
Aimed at your highness, no inveterate malice.
  K. Richard. Then call them to our presence—face
      to face,
And frowning brow to brow, ourselves will hear
The accuser and the accused freely speak:
High-stomached are they both and full of ire,
In rage, deaf as the sea, hasty as fire.

'*Enter BOLINGBROKE and MOWBRAY*'

20 *Bolingbroke*. Many years of happy days befal
  My gracious sovereign, my most loving liege!
    Mowbray. Each day still better other's happiness,
  Until the heavens, envying earth's good hap,
  Add an immortal title to your crown!
    K. Richard. We thank you both, yet one but
      flatters us,
  As well appeareth by the cause you come,
  Namely, to appeal each other of high treason:
  Cousin of Hereford, what dost thou object
  Against the Duke of Norfolk, Thomas Mowbray?
30 *Bolingbroke*. First—heaven be the record to
      my speech
  In the devotion of a subject's love,
  Tend'ring the precious safety of my prince,
  And free from other misbegotten hate,
  Come I appellant to this princely presence....
  Now Thomas Mowbray do I turn to thee,
  And mark my greeting well: for what I speak
  My body shall make good upon this earth,
  Or my divine soul answer it in heaven:
  Thou art a traitor and a miscreant,
40 Too good to be so, and too bad to live,
  Since the more fair and crystal is the sky,
  The uglier seem the clouds that in it fly:
  Once more, the more to aggravate the note,
  With a foul traitor's name stuff I thy throat,
  And wish (so please my sovereign) ere I move,
  What my tongue speaks my right drawn sword
      may prove.
    Mowbray. Let not my cold words here accuse my zeal.
  'Tis not the trial of a woman's war,

The bitter clamour of two eager tongues,
Can arbitrate this cause betwixt us twain.   50
The blood is hot that must be cooled for this.
Yet can I not of such tame patience boast
As to be hushed and nought at all to say....
First the fair reverence of your highness curbs me
From giving reins and spurs to my free speech,
Which else would post until it had returned   .
These terms of treason doubled down his throat:
Setting aside his high blood's royalty,
And let him be no kinsman to my liege,
I do defy him, and I spit at him,   60
Call him a slanderous coward, and a villain,
Which to maintain I would allow him odds,
And meet him were I tied to run afoot,
Even to the frozen ridges of the Alps,
Or any other ground inhabitable,
Where ever Englishman durst set his foot.
Mean time, let this defend my loyalty—
By all my hopes most falsely doth he lie.
    Bolingbroke. Pale trembling coward there I throw
        my gage,   *[he casts it at Mowbray's feet*
Disclaiming here the kindred of the king,   70
And lay aside my high blood's royalty,
Which fear, not reverence, makes thee to except....
If guilty dread have left thee so much strength,
As to take up mine honour's pawn, then stoop.
By that, and all the rites of knighthood else,
Will I make good against thee, arm to arm,
What I have spoke, or thou canst worse devise.
    Mowbray. I take it up, and by that sword I swear,
Which gently laid my knighthood on my shoulder,
I'll answer thee in any fair degree,   80
Or chivalrous design of knightly trial:

And when I mount, alive may I not light,
If I be traitor or unjustly fight!
   K. Richard. What doth our cousin lay to
      Mowbray's charge?
It must be great that can inherit us
So much as of a thought of ill in him.
   Bolingbroke. Look what I speak, my life shall prove
      it true,
That Mowbray hath received eight thousand nobles
In name of 'lendings' for your highness' soldiers,
90 The which he hath detained for lewd employments,
Like a false traitor, and injurious villain:
Besides I say, and will in battle prove,
Or here, or elsewhere to the furthest verge
That ever was surveyed by English eye,
That all the treasons for these eighteen years,
Complotted and contrived in this land...
Fetch from false Mowbray their first head and spring!
Further I say, and further will maintain
Upon his bad life to make all this good,
100 That he did plot the Duke of Gloucester's death,
Suggest his soon-believing adversaries,
And consequently like a traitor coward,
Sluiced out his innocent soul through streams of blood,
Which blood, like sacrificing Abel's, cries,
Even from the tongueless caverns of the earth,
To me for justice and rough chastisement:
And by the glorious worth of my descent,
This arm shall do it, or this life be spent.
   K. Richard. How high a pitch his resolution soars!
110 Thomas of Norfolk, what say'st thou to this?
   Mowbray. O, let my sovereign turn away his face,
And bid his ears a little while be deaf,
Till I have told this slander of his blood,

How God and good men hate so foul a liar.
  K. Richard. Mowbray, impartial are our eyes
      and ears,
Were he my brother, nay, my kingdom's heir,
As he is but my father's brother's son,
Now by my sceptre's awe I make a vow,
Such neighbour nearness to our sacred blood
Should nothing privilege him nor partialize   120
The unstooping firmness of my upright soul.
He is our subject, Mowbray, so art thou,
Free speech and fearless I to thee allow.
  Mowbray. Then Bolingbroke as low as to thy heart
Through the false passage of thy throat thou liest!
Three parts of that receipt I had for Calais
Disbursed I duly to his highness' soldiers,
The other part reserved I by consent,
For that my sovereign liege was in my debt,
Upon remainder of a dear account,   130
Since last I went to France to fetch his queen:
Now swallow down that lie....For Gloucester's death,
I slew him not, but to my own disgrace
Neglected my sworn duty in that case:
For you, my noble lord of Lancaster,
The honourable father to my foe,
Once did I lay an ambush for your life,
A trespass that doth vex my grievéd soul:
But ere I last received the sacrament,
I did confess it, and exactly begged   140
Your grace's pardon, and I hope I had it....
This is my fault—as for the rest appealed
It issues from the rancour of a villain,
A recreant and most degenerate traitor,
Which in myself I boldly will defend,
And interchangeably hurl down my gage

Upon this overweening traitor's foot,
To prove myself a loyal gentleman,
Even in the best blood chambered in his bosom,
150 In haste whereof most heartily I pray
Your highness to assign our trial day.

 K. Richard. Wrath-kindled gentlemen, be ruled
  by me,
Let's purge this choler without letting blood.
This we prescribe, though no physician—
Deep malice makes too deep incision—
Forget, forgive, conclude and be agreed.
Our doctors say this is no month to bleed...
Good uncle, let this end where it begun,
We'll calm the Duke of Norfolk, you your son.

160 *Gaunt.* To be a make-peace shall become my age,
Throw down, my son, the Duke of Norfolk's gage.

 K. Richard. And, Norfolk, throw down his.

 Gaunt.   When, Harry? when?
Obedience bids I should not bid again.

 K. Richard. Norfolk, throw down we bid, there is
  no boot.

 Mowbray. Myself I throw, dread sovereign, at thy foot,
My life thou shalt command, but not my shame,
The one my duty owes, but my fair name,
Despite of death that lives upon my grave,
To dark dishonour's use thou shalt not have:
170 I am disgraced, impeached, and baffled here,
Pierced to the soul with slander's venomed spear,
The which no balm can cure but his heart-blood
Which breathed this poison.

 K. Richard.   Rage must be withstood.
Give me his gage; lions make leopards tame.

 Mowbray. Yea, but not change his spots: take but
  my shame,

And I resign my gage. My dear dear lord,
The purest treasure mortal times afford,
Is spotless reputation—that away
Men are but gilded loam, or painted clay.
A jewel in a ten-times-barred-up chest   180
Is a bold spirit in a loyal breast:
Mine honour is my life, both grow in one,
Take honour from me, and my life is done:
Then, dear my liege, mine honour let me try—
In that I live, and for that will I die.
  K. Richard. Cousin, throw up your gage, do
    you begin.
  Bolingbroke. O God defend my soul from such
    deep sin!
Shall I seem crest-fallen in my father's sight?
Or with pale beggar-fear impeach my height
Before this out-dared dastard? ere my tongue   190
Shall wound my honour with such feeble wrong,
Or sound so base a parle, my teeth shall tear
The slavish motive of recanting fear,
And spit it bleeding in his high disgrace,
Where shame doth harbour, even in Mowbray's
    face.
  K. Richard. We were not born to sue, but
    to command,
Which since we cannot do, to make you friends,
Be ready, as your lives shall answer it,
At Coventry upon Saint Lambert's day.
There shall your swords and lances arbitrate   200
The swelling difference of your settled hate.
Since we can not atone you, we shall see
Justice design the victor's chivalry.
Lord marshal, command our officers at arms
Be ready to direct these home alarms.   [*they go*

[1. 2.]   *A room in the Duke of Lancaster's house*

'*Enter* JOHN OF GAUNT *with the* DUCHESS
OF GLOUCESTER'

Gaunt. Alas, the part I had in Woodstock's blood
Doth more solicit me than your exclaims
To stir against the butchers of his life,
But since correction lieth in those hands,
Which made the fault that we cannot correct...
Put we our quarrel to the will of heaven,
Who, when they see the hours ripe on earth,
Will rain hot vengeance on offenders' heads.
   Duchess. Finds brotherhood in thee no sharper spur?
10 Hath love in thy old blood no living fire?
Edward's seven sons, whereof thyself art one,
Were as seven vials of his sacred blood,
Or seven fair branches springing from one root:
Some of those seven are dried by nature's course,
Some of those branches by the Destinies cut:
But Thomas, my dear lord, my life, my Gloucester,
One vial full of Edward's sacred blood,
One flourishing branch of his most royal root,
Is cracked, and all the precious liquor spilt,
20 Is hacked down, and his summer leaves all faded,
By envy's hand, and murder's bloody axe....

                                        [*she weeps*

Ah, Gaunt, his blood was thine! that bed,
      that womb,
That mettle, that self mould, that fashioned thee
Made him a man; and though thou livest
      and breathest,
Yet art thou slain in him. Thou dost consent
In some large measure to thy father's death,

In that thou seest thy wretched brother die,
Who was the model of thy father's life...
Call it not patience, Gaunt, it is despair.
In suff'ring thus thy brother to be slaught'red,   30
Thou showest the naked pathway to thy life,
Teaching stern murder how to butcher thee:
That which in mean men we intitle patience,
Is pale cold cowardice in noble breasts....
What shall I say? to safeguard thine own life,
The best way is to venge my Gloucester's death.

  Gaunt. God's is the quarrel—for God's substitute,
His deputy anointed in His sight,
Hath caused his death, the which if wrongfully,
Let heaven revenge, for I may never lift   40
An angry arm against His minister.

  Duchess. Where then, alas, may I complain myself?

  Gaunt. To God, the widow's champion and defence.

  Duchess. Why then, I will...Farewell, old Gaunt.
Thou goest to Coventry, there to behold
Our cousin Hereford and fell Mowbray fight.
O, sit my husband's wrongs on Hereford's spear,
That it may enter butcher Mowbray's breast!
Or if misfortune miss the first career,
Be Mowbray's sins so heavy in his bosom,   50
That they may break his foaming courser's back,
And throw the rider headlong in the lists,
A caitiff recreant to my cousin Hereford!
Farewell old Gaunt, thy sometimes brother's wife
With her companion Grief must end her life.

  Gaunt. Sister farewell, I must to Coventry,
As much good stay with thee, as go with me!

  Duchess. Yet one word more—Grief boundeth where
    it falls,
Not with the empty hollowness, but weight:

60 I take my leave before I have begun,
For sorrow ends not when it seemeth done:
Commend me to thy brother, Edmund York.
Lo, this is all...nay, yet depart not so,
Though this be all, do not so quickly go...
I shall remember more...Bid him—ah, what?—
With all good speed at Plashy visit me.
Alack and what shall good old York there see
But empty lodgings and unfurnished walls,
Unpeopled offices, untrodden stones?
70 And what hear there for welcome but my groans?
Therefore commend me, let him not come there,
To seek out sorrow that dwells every where.
Desolate, desolate, will I hence and die:
The last leave of thee takes my weeping eye.   [*they go*

[1. 3.] *The lists at Coventry; to the side a platform, with
a throne (richly hanged and adorned) for the king, and
seats for his court; at either end of the lists chairs for
the combatants; a great throng of spectators. Heralds, &c.
attending*

'Enter the Lord Marshal and the DUKE AUMERLE'

Marshal. My Lord Aumerle, is Harry Hereford
    armed?
Aumerle. Yea, at all points, and longs to enter in.
Marshal. The Duke of Norfolk, sprightfully
    and bold,
Stays but the summons of the appellant's trumpet.
Aumerle. Why then, the champions are prepared
    and stay
For nothing but his majesty's approach.

The trumpets sound and the KING, bearing a truncheon,
enters with his nobles (GAUNT among them): when they
are set, enter the DUKE OF NORFOLK in arms defendant

K. Richard. Marshal, demand of yonder champion
The cause of his arrival here in arms,
Ask him his name, and orderly proceed
To swear him in the justice of his cause.   10
   Marshal. In God's name and the king's say who
     thou art,
And why thou comest thus knightly clad in arms,
Against what man thou com'st, and what thy quarrel.
Speak truly, on thy knighthood, and thy oath,
And so defend thee heaven and thy valour!
   Mowbray. My name is Thomas Mowbray, Duke
     of Norfolk,
Who hither come engagéd by my oath
(Which God defend a knight should violate!)
Both to defend my loyalty and truth,
To God, my king, and my succeeding issue,   20
Against the Duke of Hereford that appeals me,
And by the grace of God, and this mine arm,
To prove him, in defending of myself,
A traitor to my God, my king, and me—
And as I truly fight, defend me heaven!
                       [he takes his seat

The trumpets sound. Enter the DUKE
OF HEREFORD appellant in armour

K. Richard. Marshal, ask yonder knight in arms,
Both who he is, and why he cometh hither,
Thus plated in habiliments of war,
And formally, according to our law,
Depose him in the justice of his cause.   30

Marshal. What is thy name? and wherefore com'st
    thou hither,
Before King Richard in his royal lists?
Against whom comest thou? and what's thy quarrel?
Speak like a true knight, so defend thee heaven!
  Bolingbroke. Harry of Hereford, Lancaster
    and Derby
Am I, who ready here do stand in arms
To prove by God's grace, and my body's valour
In lists, on Thomas Mowbray Duke of Norfolk,
That he is a traitor foul and dangerous,
40 To God of heaven, King Richard and to me:
And as I truly fight, defend me heaven!
  Marshal. On pain of death, no person be so bold,
Or daring-hardy, as to touch the lists,
Except the marshal and such officers
Appointed to direct these fair designs.
  Bolingbroke. Lord marshal, let me kiss my
    sovereign's hand,
And bow my knee before his majesty,
For Mowbray and myself are like two men
That vow a long and weary pilgrimage,
50 Then let us take a ceremonious leave,
And loving farewell of our several friends.
  Marshal. The appellant in all duty greets your highness,
And craves to kiss your hand, and take his leave.
  K. Richard. [*rises*] We will descend and fold him in
    our arms.
Cousin of Hereford, as thy cause is right,
So be thy fortune in this royal fight...
            [*he descends with Gaunt and other nobles
                into the lists and embraces Bolingbroke*
Farewell, my blood, which if to-day thou shed,
Lament we may, but not revenge thee dead.

Bolingbroke. O, let no nòble eye profane a tear
For me, if I be gored with Mowbray's spear: 60
As confident as is the falcon's flight
Against a bird, do I with Mowbray fight....
My loving lord, [*to the Marshal*] I take my leave
  of you:
Of you, my noble cousin, Lord Aumerle—
Not sick, although I have to do with death,
But lusty, young, and cheerly drawing breath:
Lo, as at English feasts, so I regreet
The daintiest last, to make the end most sweet....
                                        [*to Gaunt*

O thou, the earthly author of my blood,
Whose youthful spirit in me regenerate   70
Doth with a twofold vigour lift me up
To reach at victory above my head...
Add proof unto mine armour with thy prayers,
And with thy blessings steel my lance's point,
That it may enter Mowbray's waxen coat,
And furbish new the name of John a Gaunt,
Even in the lusty haviour of his son.
  Gaunt. God in thy good cause make thee prosperous,
Be swift like lightning in the execution,
And let thy blows, doubly redoubled,   80
Fall like amazing thunder on the casque
Of thy adverse pernicious enemy!
Rouse up thy youthful blood, be valiant and live.
  Bolingbroke. —Mine innocency and Saint George
  to thrive!   [*he takes his seat*
  Mowbray. [*rising*] However God or fortune cast
  my lot,
There lives or dies true to King Richard's throne,
A loyal, just, and upright gentleman:
Never did captive with a freer heart

Cast off his chains of bondage, and embrace
90 His golden uncontrolled enfranchisement,
More than my dancing soul doth celebrate
This feast of battle with mine adversary.
Most mighty liege, and my companion peers,
Take from my mouth the wish of happy years:
As gentle and as jocund as to jest
Go I to fight—truth hath a quiet breast.
 K. Richard. Farewell, my lord, securely I espy
Virtue with valour couchéd in thine eye.
Order the trial, marshal, and begin.

> [*the King and his lords return to their seats;*
> *Bolingbroke and Mowbray don their helmets*
> *and lower the visors*

100 *Marshal.* Harry of Hereford, Lancaster and Derby,
Receive thy lance, and God defend the right!
 Bolingbroke. Strong as a tower in hope I cry
  'amen'.
 Marshal. [*to a knight*] Go bear this lance to Thomas,
  Duke of Norfolk.
 1 *Herald.* Harry of Hereford, Lancaster, and Derby,
Stands here, for God, his sovereign, and himself,
On pain to be found false and recreant,
To prove the Duke of Norfolk, Thomas Mowbray,
A traitor to his God, his king, and him,
And dares him to set forward to the fight.
110 2 *Herald.* Here standeth Thomas Mowbray, Duke
  of Norfolk,
On pain to be found false and recreant,
Both to defend himself, and to approve
Henry of Hereford, Lancaster, and Derby,
To God, his sovereign, and to him disloyal,
Courageously, and with a free desire,
Attending but the signal to begin.

Marshal. Sound, trumpets, and set forward,
   combatants...

'*A charge sounded.*' *The champions are about to join
battle, when the* KING *rises and casts his truncheon into
the lists*

Stay, the king hath thrown his warder down.
   K. Richard. Let them lay by their helmets and
      their spears,
And both return back to their chairs again.   120
Withdraw with us [*to the councillors about him*], and let
      the trumpets sound,
While we return these dukes what we decree....

The trumpets sound a long flourish, as the KING *and his
council retire to a room at the back of the platform; the
combatants remove their helmets and return to their chairs,
and the spectators murmur in astonishment. After some
moments, the* KING *returns and summons the combatants
to him*

Draw near
And list what with our council we have done...
For that our kingdom's earth should not be soiled
With that dear blood which it hath fosteréd;
And for our eyes do hate the dire aspect
Of civil wounds ploughed up with neighbours' sword,
And for we think the eagle-wingéd pride
Of sky-aspiring and ambitious thoughts,   130
With rival-hating envy, set on you
To wake our peace, which in our country's cradle
Draws the sweet infant breath of gentle sleep;
†Which so roused up with boist'rous untuned drums,
With harsh-resounding trumpets' dreadful bray,
And grating shock of wrathful iron arms,

Might from our quiet confines fright fair peace,
And make us wade even in our kindred's blood;
Therefore we banish you our territories:
140 You, cousin Hereford, upon pain of life,
Till twice five summers have enriched our fields,
Shall not regreet our fair dominions,
But tread the stranger paths of banishment.
　Bolingbroke. Your will be done; this must my
　　comfort be,
That sun that warms you here, shall shine on me,
And those his golden beams to you here lent,
Shall point on me, and gild my banishment.
　K. Richard. Norfolk, for thee remains a heavier doom,
Which I with some unwillingness pronounce.
150 The sly slow hours shall not determinate
The dateless limit of thy dear exile.
The hopeless word of 'never to return'
Breathe I against thee, upon pain of life.
　Mowbray. A heavy sentence, my most sovereign liege,
And all unlooked for from your highness' mouth.
A dearer merit, not so deep a maim
As to be cast forth in the common air,
Have I deservéd at your highness' hands...
The language I have learnt these forty years,
160 My native English, now I must forego,
And now my tongue's use is to me no more
Than an unstringéd viol or a harp,
Or like a cunning instrument cased up—
Or being open, put into his hands
That knows no touch to tune the harmony:
Within my mouth you have engaoled my tongue,
Doubly portcullised with my teeth and lips,
And dull unfeeling barren ignorance
Is made my gaoler to attend on me:

I am too old to fawn upon a nurse,   170
Too far in years to be a pupil now,
What is thy sentence then but speechless death,
Which robs my tongue from breathing native breath?
  K. Richard. It boots thee not to be compassionate,
After our sentence plaining comes too late.
  Mowbray. Then thus I turn me from my country's light,
To dwell in solemn shades of endless night.
                                          [*he moves away*
  K. Richard. Return again, and take an oath with thee.
Lay on our royal sword your banished hands,
Swear by the duty that you owe to God   180
(Our part therein we banish with yourselves,)
To keep the oath that we administer:
You never shall, so help you truth and God,
Embrace each other's love in banishment,
Nor never look upon each other's face,
Nor never write, regreet, nor reconcile
This louring tempest of your home-bred hate,
Nor never by advisèd purpose meet,
To plot, contrive, or complot any ill,
'Gainst us, our state, our subjects, or our land.   190
  Bolingbroke. I swear.
  Mowbray. And I, to keep all this.
  Bolingbroke. Norfolk, so fare as to mine enemy...
By this time, had the king permitted us,
One of our souls had wand'red in the air,
Banished this frail sepulchre of our flesh,
As now our flesh is banished from this land.
Confess thy treasons ere thou fly the realm—
Since thou hast far to go, bear not along
The clogging burthen of a guilty soul.   200
  Mowbray. No, Bolingbroke, if ever I were traitor,
My name be blotted from the book of life,

And I from heaven banished as from hence:
But what thou art, God, thou, and I do know,
And all too soon, I fear, the king shall rue:
Farewell, my liege. Now no way can I stray—
Save back to England all the world's my way. [*he goes*

   K. Richard. Uncle, even in the glasses of thine eyes
I see thy grievéd heart: thy sad aspect
210 Hath from the number of his banished years
Plucked four away. [*to Bolingbroke*] Six frozen
      winters spent,
Return with welcome home from banishment.

   Bolingbroke. How long a time lies in one little word!
Four lagging winters and four wanton springs
End in a word—such is the breath of kings.

   Gaunt. I thank my liege that, in regard of me,
He shortens four years of my son's exile,
But little vantage shall I reap thereby:
For, ere the six years that he hath to spend
220 Can change their moons, and bring their times about,
My oil-dried lamp and time-bewasted light
Shall be extinct with age and endless night,
My inch of taper will be burnt and done,
And blindfold Death not let me see my son.

   K. Richard. Why, uncle, thou hast many years to live.

   Gaunt. But not a minute, king, that thou canst give,
Shorten my days thou canst with sullen sorrow,
And pluck nights from me, but not lend a morrow:
Thou canst help time to furrow me with age,
230 But stop no wrinkle in his pilgrimage:
Thy word is current with him for my death,
But dead, thy kingdom cannot buy my breath.

   K. Richard. Thy son is banished upon good advice,
Whereto thy tongue a party-verdict gave,
Why at our justice seem'st thou then to lour?

Gaunt. Things sweet to taste, prove in
　　digestion sour....
You urged me as a judge, but I had rather,
You would have bid me argue like a father:
O, had it been a stranger, not my child,
To smooth his fault I should have been more mild:　　240
A partial slander sought I to avoid,
And in the sentence my own life destroyed:
Alas, I looked when some of you should say,
I was too strict to make mine own away:
But you gave leave to my unwilling tongue,
Against my will to do myself this wrong.
　K. Richard. Cousin, farewell—and uncle, bid him so,
Six years we banish him and he shall go.
　　　　['*Flourish.*' *K. Richard departs with his train*
　Aumerle. [*following*] Cousin, farewell, what presence
　　must not know,
From where you do remain let paper show.　　250
　Marshal. My lord, no leave take I, for I will ride
As far as land will let me by your side.
　Gaunt. O, to what purpose dost thou hoard thy words,
That thou returnest no greeting to thy friends?
　Bolingbroke. I have too few to take my leave of you,
When the tongue's office should be prodigal
To breathe the abundant dolour of the heart.
　Gaunt. Thy grief is but thy absence for a time.
　Bolingbroke. Joy absent, grief is present for that time.
　Gaunt. What is six winters? they are quickly gone—　　260
　Bolingbroke. To men in joy, but grief makes one
　　hour ten.
　Gaunt. Call it a travel that thou tak'st for pleasure.
　Bolingbroke. My heart will sigh when I miscall it so,
Which finds it an inforcéd pilgrimage.
　Gaunt. The sullen passage of thy weary steps

Esteem as foil wherein thou art to set
The precious jewel of thy home return.
   Bolingbroke. Nay, rather, every tedious stride I make
Will but remember me what a deal of world
270 I wander from the jewels that I love....
Must I not serve a long apprenticehood
To foreign passages, and in the end,
Having my freedom, boast of nothing else,
But that I was a journeyman to grief?
   Gaunt. All places that the eye of heaven visits
Are to a wise man ports and happy havens:
Teach thy necessity to reason thus—
There is no virtue like necessity.
Think not the king did banish thee,
280 But thou the king....Woe doth the heavier sit,
Where it perceives it is but faintly borne:
Go, say I sent thee forth to purchase honour,
And not the king exiled thee; or suppose
Devouring pestilence hangs in our air,
And thou art flying to a fresher clime:
Look, what thy soul holds dear, imagine it
To lie that way thou goest, not whence thou com'st:
Suppose the singing birds musicians,
The grass whereon thou tread'st the presence strewed,
290 The flowers fair ladies, and thy steps no more
Than a delightful measure or a dance,
For gnarling sorrow hath less power to bite
The man that mocks at it and sets it light.
   Bolingbroke. O, who can hold a fire in his hand
By thinking on the frosty Caucasus?
Or cloy the hungry edge of appetite
By bare imagination of a feast?
Or wallow naked in December snow
By thinking on fantastic summer's heat?

O no, the apprehension of the good   300
Gives but the greater feeling to the worse:
Fell sorrow's tooth doth never rankle more
Than when he bites, but lanceth not the sore.

  Gaunt. Come, come, my son, I'll bring thee on
    thy way,
Had I thy youth and cause, I would not stay.

  Bolingbroke. Then England's ground farewell, sweet
    soil adieu,
My mother and my nurse that bears me yet!
Where'er I wander boast of this I can,
Though banished, yet a trueborn Englishman.

                          [they go

[1. 4.]   *The court*

'Enter the KING*' with* BAGOT *and* GREEN *'at one door,
and the* LORD AUMERLE *at another'*

  K. Richard. We did observe....Cousin Aumerle,
How far brought you high Hereford on his way?

  Aumerle. I brought high Hereford, if you call him so,
But to the next highway, and there I left him.

  K. Richard. And say, what store of parting tears
    were shed?

  Aumerle. Faith, none for me, except the north-east wind
Which then blew bitterly against our faces,
Awaked the sleeping rheum, and so by chance
Did grace our hollow parting with a tear.

  K. Richard. What said our cousin when you parted
    with him?   10

  Aumerle. 'Farewell'—
And for my heart disdainéd that my tongue
Should so profane the word, that taught me craft
To counterfeit oppression of such grief

That words seemed buried in my sorrow's grave:
Marry, would the word 'farewell' have length'ned hours,
And added years to his short banishment,
He should have had a volume of farewells:
But since it would not, he had none of me.
20   *K. Richard.* He is our cousin's cousin, but 'tis doubt,
When time shall call him home from banishment,
Whether our kinsman come to see his friends....
Ourself and Bushy
Observed his courtship to the common people,
How he did seem to dive into their hearts,
With humble and familiar courtesy,
What reverence he did throw away on slaves,
Wooing poor craftsmen with the craft of smiles
And patient underbearing of his fortune,
30 As 'twere to banish their affects with him.
Off goes his bonnet to an oyster-wench,
A brace of draymen bid God speed him well,
And had the tribute of his supple knee,
With 'Thanks, my countrymen, my loving friends'—
As were our England in reversion his,
And he our subjects' next degree in hope.
  Green. Well, he is gone; and with him go
    these thoughts.
Now for the rebels which stand out in Ireland,
Expedient manage must be made, my liege,
40 Ere further leisure yield them further means
For their advantage and your highness' loss.
  K. Richard. We will ourself in person to this war,
And for our coffers with too great a court
And liberal largess are grown somewhat light,
We are inforced to farm our royal realm,
The revenue whereof shall furnish us
For our affairs in hand—if that come short,

Our substitutes at home shall have blank charters,
Whereto, when they shall know what men are rich,
They shall subscribe them for large sums of gold,   50
And send them after to supply our wants,
For we will make for Ireland presently....

BUSHY enters

What news?
    Bushy. Old John of Gaunt is grievous sick, my lord,
Suddenly taken, and hath sent post haste
To entreat your majesty to visit him.
    K. Richard. Where lies he?
    Bushy. At Ely House.
    K. Richard. Now put it, God, in the physician's mind,
To help him to his grave immediately!   60
The lining of his coffers shall make coats
To deck our soldiers for these Irish wars....
Come, gentlemen, let's all go visit him,
Pray God we may make haste and come too late!
    All. Amen.   [*they go out*

[2. 1.]   *Ely House*

'*Enter JOHN OF GAUNT sick*' *borne in a chair,*
    '*with the DUKE OF YORK, &c.*'

Gaunt. Will the king come that I may breathe my last
In wholesome counsel to his unstaid youth?
    York. Vex not yourself, nor strive not with your breath,
For all in vain comes counsel to his ear.
    Gaunt. O, but they say the tongues of dying men
Enforce attention like deep harmony:
Where words are scarce they are seldom spent in vain,
For they breathe truth that breathe their words in pain:

He that no more must say is listened more
10 Than they whom youth and ease have taught to glose,
More are men's ends marked than their lives before:
The setting sun, and music at the close,
As the last taste of sweets, is sweetest last,
Writ in remembrance more than things long past.
Though Richard my life's counsel would not hear,
My death's sad tale may yet undeaf his ear.
  York. No, it is stopped with other flattering sounds,
  †As praises, of whose taste the wise are fond,
Lascivious metres, to whose venom sound
20 The open ear of youth doth always listen,
Report of fashions in proud Italy,
Whose manners still our tardy apish nation
Limps after in base imitation:
Where doth the world thrust forth a vanity—
So it be new, there's no respect how vile—
That is not quickly buzzed into his ears?
Then all too late comes counsel to be heard,
Where will doth mutiny with wit's regard:
Direct not him whose way himself will choose,
30 'Tis breath thou lack'st, and that breath wilt thou lose.
  Gaunt. Methinks I am a prophet new inspired—
And thus expiring do foretell of him—
His rash fierce blaze of riot cannot last;
For violent fires soon burn out themselves,
Small showers last long, but sudden storms are short:
He tires betimes that spurs too fast betimes:
With eager feeding food doth choke the feeder:
Light vanity, insatiate cormorant,
Consuming means, soon preys upon itself:
40 This royal throne of kings, this sceptered isle,
This earth of majesty, this seat of Mars,
This other Eden, demi-paradise,

This fortress built by nature for herself
Against infection and the hand of war,
This happy breed of men, this little world,
This precious stone set in the silver sea,
Which serves it in the office of a wall,
Or as a moat defensive to a house,
Against the envy of less happier lands....
This blessed plot, this earth, this realm, this England,   50
This nurse, this teeming womb of royal kings,
Feared by their breed, and famous by their birth,
Renownéd for their deeds as far from home,
For Christian service and true chivalry,
As is the sepulchre in stubborn Jewry
Of the world's ransom, blessed Mary's Son:
This land of such dear souls, this dear dear land,
Dear for her reputation through the world,
Is now leased out—I die pronouncing it—
Like to a tenement or pelting farm....   60
England, bound in with the triumphant sea,
Whose rocky shore beats back the envious siege
Of wat'ry Neptune, is now bound in with shame,
With inky blots, and rotten parchment bonds:
That England, that was wont to conquer others,
Hath made a shameful conquest of itself:
Ah, would the scandal vanish with my life,
How happy then were my ensuing death!

'*Enter* KING, QUEEN, AUMERLE, BUSHY, GREEN,
BAGOT, ROSS, *and* WILLOUGHBY'

York. The king is come, deal mildly with his youth,
†For young hot colts, being ragged, do rage the more.   70
Queen. How fares our noble uncle, Lancaster?
K. Richard. What comfort, man? how is't with
    aged Gaunt?

Gaunt. O, how that name befits my composition!
Old Gaunt indeed, and gaunt in being old:
Within me grief hath kept a tedious fast,
And who abstains from meat that is not gaunt?
For sleeping England long time have I watched,
Watching breeds leanness, leanness is all gaunt:
The pleasure that some fathers feed upon
80 Is my strict fast; I mean my children's looks,
And therein fasting hast thou made me gaunt:
Gaunt am I for the grave, gaunt as a grave,
Whose hollow womb inherits nought but bones.
　　K. Richard. Can sick men play so nicely with
　　　　their names?
　　Gaunt. No, misery makes sport to mock itself—
Since thou dost seek to kill my name in me,
I mock my name, great king, to flatter thee.
　　K. Richard. Should dying men flatter with those
　　　　that live?
　　Gaunt. No, no, men living flatter those that die.
90　*K. Richard.* Thou now a-dying sayest thou
　　　　flatterest me.
　　Gaunt. Oh no, thou diest, though I the sicker be.
　　K. Richard. I am in health, I breathe, and see thee ill.
　　Gaunt. Now He that made me knows I see thee ill,
Ill in myself to see, and in thee, seeing ill.
Thy death-bed is no lesser than thy land,
Wherein thou liest in reputation sick,
And thou too careless patient as thou art
Commit'st thy anointed body to the cure
Of those physicians that first wounded thee.
100 A thousand flatterers sit within thy crown,
Whose compass is no bigger than thy head,
And yet incagéd in so small a verge,
The waste is no whit lesser than thy land:

O, had thy grandsire with a prophet's eye
Seen how his son's son should destroy his sons,
From forth thy reach he would have laid thy shame,
Deposing thee before thou wert possessed,
Which art possessed now to depose thyself:
Why, cousin, wert thou regent of the world,
It were a shame to let this land by lease: 110
But for thy world enjoying but this land,
Is it not more than shame to shame it so?
Landlord of England art thou now, not king,
Thy state of law is bondslave to the law,
And thou—
   K. Richard.   A lunatic lean-witted fool,
Presuming on an ague's privilege,
Darest with thy frozen admonition
Make pale our cheek, chasing the royal blood
With fury from his native residence....
Now by my seat's right royal majesty,   120
Wert thou not brother to great Edward's son,
This tongue that runs so roundly in thy head
Should run thy head from thy unreverent shoulders.
   Gaunt. O, spare me not, my brother Edward's son,
For that I was his father Edward's son,
That blood already, like the pelican,
Hast thou tapped out and drunkenly caroused.
My brother Gloucester, plain well-meaning soul,
Whom fair befal in heaven 'mongst happy souls,
May be a precedent and witness good...   130
That thou respect'st not spilling Edward's blood!
Join with the present sickness that I have,
And thy unkindness be like crooked age,
To crop at once a too long withered flower.
Live in thy shame, but die not shame with thee!
These words hereafter thy tormentors be!

Convey me to my bed, then to my grave—
Love they to live that love and honour have.

             [*he is borne out by attendants*

    K. Richard. And let them die that age and sullens have,
140 For both hast thou, and both become the grave.

    York. I do beseech your majesty, impute his words
To wayward sickliness and age in him.
He loves you, on my life, and holds you dear
As Harry Duke of Hereford, were he here.

    K. Richard. Right, you say true—as Hereford's love, so his,
As theirs, so mine, and all be as it is.

NORTHUMBERLAND *enters*

    Northumberland. My liege, old Gaunt commends him
       to your majesty.

    K. Richard. What says he?

    Northumberland.   Nay nothing, all is said:
His tongue is now a stringless instrument,
150 Words, life, and all, old Lancaster hath spent.

    York. Be York the next that must be bankrupt so!
Though death be poor, it ends a mortal woe.

    K. Richard. The ripest fruit first falls, and so doth he,
His time is spent, our pilgrimage must be;
So much for that....Now for our Irish wars—
We must supplant those rough rug-headed kerns,
Which live like venom, where no venom else
But only they have privilege to live.
And for these great affairs do ask some charge,
160 Towards our assistance we do seize to us...
The plate, coin, revenues, and moveables,
Whereof our uncle Gaunt did stand possessed.

         [*he goes about the room, rating the costly objects therein*

    York. How long shall I be patient? ah, how long

Shall tender duty make me suffer wrong?
Not Gloucester's death, nor Hereford's banishment,
Not Gaunt's rebukes, nor England's private wrongs,
Nor the prevention of poor Bolingbroke
About his marriage, nor my own disgrace,
Have ever made me sour my patient cheek,
Or bend one wrinkle on my sovereign's face: 170
I am the last of noble Edward's sons,
Of whom thy father, Prince of Wales, was first.
In war was never lion raged more fierce,
In peace was never gentle lamb more mild,
Than was that young and princely gentleman:
His face thou hast, for even so looked he,
Accomplished with the number of thy hours;
But when he frowned it was against the French,
And not against his friends; his noble hand
Did win what he did spend, and spent not that   180
Which his triumphant father's hand had won:
His hands were guilty of no kindred blood,
But bloody with the enemies of his kin:
O, Richard...York is too far gone with grief,
Or else he never would compare between....
                                    [*he sobs aloud*
  K. Richard. [*turns*] Why, uncle, what's the matter?
  York.   O, my liege,
Pardon me, if you please—if not, I pleased
Not to be pardoned, am content withal.
Seek you to seize and gripe into your hands
The royalties and rights of banished Hereford?   190
Is not Gaunt dead? and doth not Hereford live?
Was not Gaunt just? and is not Harry true?
Did not the one deserve to have an heir?
Is not his heir a well-deserving son?
Take Hereford's rights away, and take from Time

                                          3-2

His charters and his customary rights;
Let not to-morrow then ensue to-day;
Be not thyself....for how art thou a king
But by fair sequence and succession?
200 Now, afore God—God forbid I say true!—
If you do wrongfully seize Hereford's rights,
Call in the letters-patents that he hath
By his attorneys-general to sue
His livery, and deny his off'red homage,
You pluck a thousand dangers on your head,
You lose a thousand well-disposéd hearts,
And prick my tender patience to those thoughts
Which honour and allegiance cannot think.
   K. Richard. Think what you will, we seize into
     our hands
210 His plate, his goods, his money and his lands.
   York. I'll not be by the while—my liege, farewell—
What will ensue hereof there's none can tell:
But by bad courses may be understood,
That their events can never fall out good.   *[he goes*
   K. Richard. Go, Bushy, to the Earl of Wiltshire straight,
Bid him repair to us to Ely House,
To see this business: to-morrow next
We will for Ireland, and 'tis time, I trow.
And we create, in absence of ourself,
220 Our uncle York lord governor of England;
For he is just, and always loved us well...
Come on, our queen, to-morrow must we part,
Be merry, for our time of stay is short.
               [he leads out the Queen, followed by
                 Bushy, Aumerle, Green, and Bagot
  Northumberland. Well, lords, the Duke of Lancaster
    is dead.
  Ross. And living too, for now his son is duke.

Willoughby. Barely in title, not in revenues.
Northumberland. Richly in both, if justice had
　　her right.
Ross. My heart is great, but it must break with silence,
Ere't be disburdened with a liberal tongue.
Northumberland. Nay, speak thy mind, and let him
　　ne'er speak more　　　　　　　　　　　　　　　　230
That speaks thy words again to do thee harm.
　Willoughby. Tends that thou wouldst speak to the
　　Duke of Hereford?
If it be so, out with it boldly, man.
Quick is mine ear to hear of good towards him.
　Ross. No good at all that I can do for him,
Unless you call it good to pity him,
Bereft, and gelded of his patrimony.
　Northumberland. Now afore God 'tis shame such
　　wrongs are borne
In him, a royal prince, and many moe
Of noble blood in this declining land.　　　　　　　240
The king is not himself, but basely led
By flatterers, and what they will inform,
Merely in hate, 'gainst any of us all,
That will the king severely prosecute
'Gainst us, our lives, our children, and our heirs.
　Ross. The commons hath he pilled with grievous taxes,
†And quite lost their hearts. The nobles hath he fined
For ancient quarrels, and quite lost their hearts.
　Willoughby. And daily new exactions are devised,
As blanks, benevolences, and I wot not what:　　　250
But what a God's name doth become of this?
　Northumberland. Wars hath not wasted it, for warred
　　he hath not,
But basely yielded upon compromise
That which his noble ancestors achieved with blows.

More hath he spent in peace than they in wars.

Ross. The Earl of Wiltshire hath the realm in farm.

Willoughby. The king's grown bankrupt like a
broken man.

Northumberland. Reproach and dissolution hangeth
over him.

Ross. He hath not money for these Irish wars,
260 His burthenous taxations notwithstanding,
But by the robbing of the banished duke.

Northumberland. His noble kinsman—most
degenerate king!
But, lords, we hear this fearful tempest sing,
Yet seek no shelter to avoid the storm:
We see the wind sit sore upon our sails,
And yet we strike not, but securely perish.

Ross. We see the very wrack that we must suffer,
And unavoided is the danger now,
For suffering so the causes of our wrack.

270 *Northumberland.* Not so, even through the hollow eyes
of death
I spy life peering, but I dare not say
How near the tidings of our comfort is.

Willoughby. Nay, let us share thy thoughts as thou
dost ours.

Ross. Be confident to speak, Northumberland,
We three are but thyself, and speaking so
Thy words are but as thoughts, therefore be bold.

Northumberland. Then thus—I have from le
Port Blanc,
A bay in Britain, received intelligence
That Harry Duke of Hereford, Rainold Lord Cobham,
280 [The son of Richard Earl of Arundel,]
That late broke from the Duke of Exeter,
His brother, Archbishop late of Canterbury,

Sir Thomas Erpingham, Sir John Ramston,
Sir John Norbery, Sir Robert Waterton and
    Francis Coint;
All these, well furnished by the Duke of Britain,
With eight tall ships, three thousand men of war,
Are making hither with all due expedience,
And shortly mean to touch our northern shore:
Perhaps they had ere this, but that they stay
The first departing of the king for Ireland....   290
If then we shall shake off our slavish yoke,
Imp out our drooping country's broken wing,
Redeem from broking pawn the blemished crown,
Wipe off the dust that hides our sceptre's gilt,
And make high majesty look like itself,
Away with me in post to Ravenspurgh:
But if you faint, as fearing to do so,
Stay, and be secret, and myself will go.
    Ross. To horse, to horse! urge doubts to them that fear.
    Willoughby. Hold out my horse, and I will first   300
        be there.   [*they hurry forth*

[2. 2.]   *Windsor Castle*

        '*Enter the* QUEEN, BUSHY, *and* BAGOT'

    Bushy. Madam, your majesty is too much sad.
You promised, when you parted with the king,
To lay aside life-harming heaviness,
And entertain a cheerful disposition.
    Queen. To please the king I did—to please myself
I cannot do it; yet I know no cause
Why I should welcome such a guest as grief,
Save bidding farewell to so sweet a guest
As my sweet Richard: yet again methinks

10 Some unborn sorrow ripe in Fortune's womb
   Is coming towards me, and my inward soul
   †With nothing trembles, yet at something grieves,
   More than with parting from my lord the king.
     Bushy. Each substance of a grief hath twenty shadows,
   Which shows like grief itself, but is not so:
   For Sorrow's eye glazéd with blinding tears,
   Divides one thing entire to many objects,
   Like perspectives, which rightly gazed upon
   Show nothing but confusion; eyed awry,
20 Distinguish form: so your sweet majesty,
   Looking awry upon your lord's departure,
   Find shapes of grief more than himself to wail,
   Which looked on as it is, is nought but shadows
   Of what it is not; then, thrice-gracious queen,
   More than your lord's departure weep not—more is
       not seen,
   Or if it be, 'tis with false Sorrow's eye,
   Which, for things true, weeps things imaginary.
     Queen. It may be so; but yet my inward soul
   Persuades me it is otherwise: howe'er it be,
30 I cannot but be sad; so heavy sad,
   As, though on thinking on no thought I think,
   Makes me with heavy nothing faint and shrink.
     Bushy. 'Tis nothing but conceit, my gracious lady.
     Queen. 'Tis nothing less: conceit is still derived
   From some forefather grief. Mine is not so,
   For nothing hath begot my something grief,
   Or something hath the nothing that I grieve—
   'Tis in reversion that I do possess—
   But what it is that is not yet known, what
40 I cannot name, 'tis nameless woe I wot.

GREEN enters

Green. God save your majesty! and well
    met, gentlemen.
I hope the king is not yet shipped for Ireland.
  Queen. Why hopest thou so? 'tis better hope he is,
For his designs crave haste, his haste good hope:
Then wherefore dost thou hope he is not shipped?
  Green. That he, our hope, might have retired
    his power,
And driven into despair an enemy's hope,
Who strongly hath set footing in this land.
The banished Bolingbroke repeals himself,
And with uplifted arms is safe arrived   50
At Ravenspurgh.
  Queen.   Now God in heaven forbid!
  Green. Ah madam, 'tis too true, and that is worse...
The Lord Northumberland, his son young Henry Percy,
The Lords of Ross, Beaumond, and Willoughby,
With all their powerful friends, are fled to him.
  Bushy. Why have you not proclaimed Northumberland
And all the rest revolted faction traitors?
  Green. We have, whereupon the Earl of Worcester
Hath broken his staff, resigned his stewardship,
And all the household servants fled with him   60
To Bolingbroke.
  Queen. So, Green, thou art the midwife to my woe,
And Bolingbroke my sorrow's dismal heir.
Now hath my soul brought forth her prodigy,
And I, a gasping new-delivered mother,
Have woe to woe, sorrow to sorrow joined.
  Bushy. Despair not, madam.
  Queen.   Who shall hinder me?
I will despair, and be at enmity

With cozening Hope—he is a flatterer,
70 A parasite, a keeper back of Death,
Who gently would dissolve the bands of life,
Which false Hope lingers in extremity.

YORK enters with his gorget on

   Green. Here comes the Duke of York.
   Queen. With signs of war about his aged neck.
O, full of careful business are his looks!
Uncle, for God's sake, speak comfortable words.
   York. Should I do so, I should belie my thoughts.
Comfort's in heaven, and we are on the earth,
Where nothing lives but crosses, cares, and grief:
80 Your husband he is gone to save far off,
Whilst others come to make him lose at home:
Here am I left to underprop his land,
Who weak with age cannot support myself.
Now comes the sick hour that his surfeit made,
Now shall he try his friends that flattered him.

A servingman enters

   Servingman. My lord, your son was gone before
     I came.
   York. He was? Why, so! go all which way it will!
†The nobles they are fled, the commons cold,
And will, I fear, revolt on Hereford's side....
90 Sirrah,
Get thee to Plashy, to my sister Gloucester,
Bid her send me presently a thousand pound.
Hold, take my ring.
   Servingman. My lord, I had forgot to tell
     your lordship:
To-day as I came by I calléd there—
But I shall grieve you to report the rest.

York. What is't, knave?

Servingman. An hour before I came the duchess died.

York. God for his mercy, what a tide of woes

Comes rushing on this woeful land at once!   100

I know not what to do: I would to God

(So my untruth had not provoked him to it)

The king had cut off my head with my brother's....

What, are there no posts dispatched for Ireland?

How shall we do for money for these wars?

Come, sister—cousin, I would say, pray pardon me:

Go, fellow, get thee home, provide some carts,

And bring away the armour that is there....

                                        [the servingman goes

Gentlemen, will you go muster men?

If I know   110

How or which way to order these affairs,

Thus thrust disorderly into my hands,

Never believe me...Both are my kinsmen—

Th'one is my sovereign, whom both my oath

And duty bids defend; th'other again

Is my kinsman, whom the king hath wronged,

Whom conscience and my kindred bids to right....

Well, somewhat we must do....Come, cousin, I'll

Dispose of you:

Gentlemen, go, muster up your men,   120

And meet me presently at Berkeley:

I should to Plashy too,

But time will not permit: all is uneven,

And every thing is left at six and seven.

                                [he leads the Queen forth

Bushy. The wind sits fair for news to go to Ireland,

But none returns. For us to levy power

Proportionable to the enemy

Is all unpossible.

    Green. Besides, our nearness to the king in love
130 Is near the hate of those love not the king.
    Bagot. And that is the wavering commons, for their love
Lies in their purses, and whoso empties them,
By so much fills their hearts with deadly hate.
    Bushy. Wherein the king stands generally condemned.
    Bagot. If judgement lie in them, then so do we,
Because we ever have been near the king.
    Green. Well, I will for refuge straight to Bristol Castle—
The Earl of Wiltshire is already there.
    Bushy. Thither will I with you, for little office
140 The hateful commons will perform for us,
Except like curs to tear us all to pieces:
Will you go along with us?
    Bagot. No, I will to Ireland to his majesty.
Farewell—if heart's presages be not vain,
We three here part that ne'er shall meet again.
    Bushy. That's as York thrives to beat back Bolingbroke.
    Green. Alas, poor duke! the task he undertakes
Is numb'ring sands, and drinking oceans dry—
Where one on his side fights, thousands will fly:
150 Farewell at once, for once, for all, and ever.
    Bushy. Well, we may meet again.
    Bagot.   I fear me, never.
                                       [they go

[2. 3.]   *Near Berkeley Castle*

BOLINGBROKE *and* NORTHUMBERLAND, *marching
with forces up a hill*

    Bolingbroke. How far is it, my lord, to Berkeley now?
    Northumberland. Believe me, noble lord,
I am a stranger here in Gloucestershire.

These high wild hills and rough uneven ways
Draws out our miles and makes them wearisome,
And yet your fair discourse hath been as sugar,
Making the hard way sweet and delectable.
But I bethink me what a weary way
From Ravenspurgh to Cotswold will be found
In Ross and Willoughby, wanting your company,　　10
Which I protest hath very much beguiled
The tediousness and process of my travel:
But theirs is sweet'ned with the hope to have
The present benefit which I possess,
And hope to joy is little less in joy
Than hope enjoyed: by this the weary lords
Shall make their way seem short, as mine hath done
By sight of what I have, your noble company.
　　Bolingbroke. Of much less value is my company
Than your good words....But who comes here?　　20

HARRY PERCY comes over the crest of the hill

　　Northumberland. It is my son, young Harry Percy,
Sent from my brother Worcester, whencesoever....
Harry, how fares your uncle?
　　Percy. I had thought, my lord, to have learned his
　　　　health of you.
　　Northumberland. Why, is he not with the queen?
　　Percy. No, my good lord, he hath forsook the court,
Broken his staff of office, and dispersed
The household of the king.
　　Northumberland.　　　　What was his reason?
He was not so resolved, when last we spake together.
　　Percy. Because your lordship was proclaiméd traitor.　30
But he, my lord, is gone to Ravenspurgh,
To offer service to the Duke of Hereford,
And sent me over by Berkeley to discover

What power the Duke of York had levied there,
Then with directions to repair to Ravenspurgh.

   Northumberland. Have you forgot the Duke of
      Hereford, boy?

   Percy. No, my good lord, for that is not forgot
Which ne'er I did remember—to my knowledge
I never in my life did look on him.

40 *Northumberland.* Then learn to know him now. This
      is the duke.

   Percy. My gracious lord, I tender you my service,
Such as it is, being tender, raw, and young,
Which elder days shall ripen and confirm
To more approvéd service and desert.

   Bolingbroke. I thank thee, gentle Percy, and be sure
I count myself in nothing else so happy
As in a soul rememb'ring my good friends,
And as my fortune ripens with thy love,
It shall be still thy true love's recompense.

50 My heart this covenant makes, my hand thus seals it.

   Northumberland. How far is it to Berkeley? And
      what stir
Keeps good old York there with his men of war?

   Percy. There stands the castle, by yon tuft of trees,
Manned with three hundred men, as I have heard,
And in it are the Lords of York, Berkeley, and Seymour—
None else of name and noble estimate.

Ross *and* WILLOUGHBY *come up*

   Northumberland. Here come the Lords of Ross
      and Willoughby,
Bloody with spurring, fiery-red with haste.

   Bolingbroke. Welcome, my lords. I wot your
      love pursues
60 A banished traitor: all my treasury

Is yet but unfelt thanks, which more enriched
Shall be your love and labour's recompense.
  Ross. Your presence makes us rich, most noble lord.
  Willoughby. And far surmounts our labour to attain it.
  Bolingbroke. Evermore thank's the exchequer of
       the poor,
Which till my infant fortune comes to years,
Stands for my bounty: but who comes here?

BERKELEY *approaches*

  Northumberland. It is my Lord of Berkeley, as I guess.
  Berkeley. My Lord of Hereford, my message is to you.
  Bolingbroke. My lord, my answer is to 'Lancaster',   70
And I am come to seek that name in England,
And I must find that title in your tongue,
Before I make reply to aught you say.
  Berkeley. Mistake me not, my lord, 'tis not
       my meaning
To raze one title of your honour out:
To you, my lord, I come, what lord you will,
From the most gracious regent of this land,
The Duke of York; to know what pricks you on
To take advantage of the absent time,
And fright our native peace with self-borne arms.   80

YORK *with a retinue draws near*

  Bolingbroke. I shall not need transport my words
       by you,
Here comes his grace in person.
                         My noble uncle! [*he kneels*
  York. Show me thy humble heart, and not thy knee,
Whose duty is deceivable and false.
  Bolingbroke. My gracious uncle!
  York. Tut, tut!

Grace me no grace, nor uncle me no uncle,
I am no traitor's uncle, and that word 'grace'
In an ungracious mouth is but profane:
90 Why have those banished and forbidden legs
Dared once to touch a dust of England's ground?
But then more 'why?' why have they dared to march
So many miles upon her peaceful bosom,
Frighting her pale-faced villages with war,
And ostentation of despiséd arms?
Com'st thou because the anointed king is hence?
Why, foolish boy, the king is left behind,
And in my loyal bosom lies his power.
Were I but now the lord of such hot youth,
100 As when brave Gaunt, thy father, and myself,
Rescued the Black Prince, that young Mars of men,
From forth the ranks of many thousand French,
O, then how quickly should this arm of mine,
Now prisoner to the palsy, chastise thee,
And minister correction to thy fault!
  Bolingbroke. My gracious uncle, let me know my fault,
On what condition stands it and wherein?
  York. Even in condition of the worst degree—
In gross rebellion and detested treason.
110 Thou art a banished man, and here art come,
Before the expiration of thy time,
In braving arms against thy sovereign.
  Bolingbroke. As I was banished, I was
        banished Hereford,
But as I come, I come for Lancaster....
And, noble uncle, I beseech your grace
Look on my wrongs with an indifferent eye:
You are my father, for methinks in you
I see old Gaunt alive....O then my father,
Will you permit that I shall stand condemned

A wandering vagabond, my rights and royalties   120
Plucked from my arms perforce...and given away
To upstart unthrifts? Wherefore was I born?
If that my cousin king be king in England,
It must be granted I am Duke of Lancaster:
You have a son, Aumerle, my noble cousin,
Had you first died, and he been thus trod down,
He should have found his uncle Gaunt a father,
To rouse his wrongs and chase them to the bay....
I am denied to sue my livery here,
And yet my letters-patents give me leave....   130
My father's goods are all distrained and sold,
And these and all are all amiss employed....
What would you have me do? I am a subject;
And I challenge law. Attorneys are denied me,
And therefore personally I lay my claim
To my inheritance of free descent.

   Northumberland. The noble duke hath been too
     much abused.

   Ross. It stands your grace upon to do him right.

   Willoughby. Base men by his endowments are
     made great.

   York. My lords of England, let me tell you this: 140
I have had feeling of my cousin's wrongs,
And laboured all I could to do him right:
But in this kind to come, in braving arms,
Be his own carver and cut out his way,
To find out right with wrong, it may not be:
And you that do abet him in this kind
Cherish rebellion, and are rebels all.

   Northumberland. The noble duke hath sworn his
     coming is
But for his own; and for the right of that
We all have strongly sworn to give him aid: 150

And let him never see joy that breaks that oath.
   York. Well, well, I see the issue of these arms.
I cannot mend it, I must needs confess,
Because my power is weak and all ill left:
But if I could, by Him that gave me life,
I would attach you all, and make you stoop
Unto the sovereign mercy of the king;
But, since I cannot, be it known unto you,
I do remain as neuter. So, fare you well,
160 Unless you please to enter in the castle,
And there repose you for this night.
   Bolingbroke. An offer, uncle, that we will accept.
But we must win your grace to go with us
To Bristow castle, which, they say, is held
By Bushy, Bagot, and their complices,
The caterpillars of the commonwealth,
Which I have sworn to weed and pluck away.
   York. It may be I will go with you—but yet I'll pause,
For I am loath to break our country's laws.
170 Nor friends nor foes, to me welcome you are:
Things past redress are now with me past care.

                              [they go forward

[2. 4.]   *A camp in Wales*

        SALISBURY, *and a Welsh Captain*

   Captain. My Lord of Salisbury, we have stayed
     ten days,
And hardly kept our countrymen together,
And yet we hear no tidings from the king,
Therefore we will disperse ourselves. Farewell.
   Salisbury. Stay yet another day, thou trusty Welshman.
The king reposeth all his confidence in thee.

Captain. 'Tis thought the king is dead; we will
    not stay.
The bay-trees in our country are all withered,
And meteors fright the fixéd stars of heaven,
The pale-faced moon looks bloody on the earth,   10
And lean-looked prophets whisper fearful change,
Rich men look sad, and ruffians dance and leap—
The one in fear to lose what they enjoy,
The other to enjoy by rage and war:
These signs forerun the death or fall of kings....
Farewell. Our countrymen are gone and fled,
As well assured Richard their king is dead.   [*he goes*
  Salisbury. Ah, Richard! with the eyes of heavy mind
I see thy glory like a shooting star
Fall to the base earth from the firmament.   20
Thy sun sets weeping in the lowly west,
Witnessing storms to come, woe, and unrest.
Thy friends are fled to wait upon thy foes,
And crossly to thy good all fortune goes.   [*he goes*

[3. 1.]   *Bristol. Before the castle*

Enter BOLINGBROKE, YORK, NORTHUMBERLAND,
    with BUSHY *and* GREEN, *prisoners*

  Bolingbroke. Bring forth these men....
Bushy and Green, I will not vex your souls,
Since presently your souls must part your bodies,
With too much urging your pernicious lives,
For 'twere no charity; yet to wash your blood
From off my hands, here in the view of men,
I will unfold some causes of your deaths:
You have misled a prince, a royal king,

A happy gentleman in blood and lineaments,
10 By you unhappied and disfigured clean.
  You have in manner with your sinful hours
  Made a divorce betwixt his queen and him,
  Broke the possession of a royal bed,
  And stained the beauty of a fair queen's cheeks
  With tears, drawn from her eyes by your foul wrongs.
  Myself, a prince by fortune of my birth,
  Near to the king in blood, and near in love,
  Till you did make him misinterpret me,
  Have stooped my neck under your injuries,
20 And sighed my English breath in foreign clouds,
  Eating the bitter bread of banishment,
  Whilst you have fed upon my signories,
  Disparked my parks, and felled my forest woods;
  From my own windows torn my household coat,
  Razed out my imprese, leaving me no sign,
  Save men's opinions and my living blood,
  To show the world I am a gentleman....
  This and much more, much more than twice all this,
  Condemns you to the death...See them delivered over
30 To execution and the hand of death.
    Bushy. More welcome is the stroke of death to me
  Than Bolingbroke to England. Lords, farewell.
    Green. My comfort is, that heaven will take our souls,
  And plague injustice with the pains of hell.
    Bolingbroke. My Lord Northumberland, see
        them dispatched...
    [*Northumberland and others depart with the prisoners*
  Uncle, you say, the queen is at your house,
  For God's sake fairly let her be entreated,
  Tell her I send to her my kind commends;
  Take special care my greetings be delivered.
40 *York.* A gentleman of mine I have dispatched

With letters of your love to her at large.
  Bolingbroke. Thanks, gentle uncle…Come,
    lords, away,
To fight with Glendower and his complices.
Awhile to work, and after holiday.   [*they go*

[3. 2.]   *Near the coast of Wales*

*KING RICHARD, the BISHOP OF CARLISLE, AUMERLE,
   and Soldiers, newly disembarked*

  K. Richard. Barkloughly castle call they this at hand?
  Aumerle. Yea, my lord. How brooks your grace
    the air,
After your late tossing on the breaking seas?
  K. Richard. Needs must I like it well. I weep for joy
To stand upon my kingdom once again:
  [*he sits upon a bank, caressing the grass with his hand*
Dear earth, I do salute thee with my hand,
Though rebels wound thee with their horses' hoofs:
As a long-parted mother with her child
Plays fondly with her tears and smiles in meeting;
So, weeping, smiling, greet I thee, my earth,   10
And do thee favours with my royal hands;
Feed not thy sovereign's foe, my gentle earth,
Nor with thy sweets comfort his ravenous sense,
But let thy spiders that suck up thy venom
And heavy-gaited toads lie in their way,
Doing annoyance to the treacherous feet,
Which with usurping steps do trample thee.
Yield stinging nettles to mine enemies:
And when they from thy bosom pluck a flower,
Guard it, I pray thee, with a lurking adder,   20
Whose double tongue may with a mortal touch

Throw death upon thy sovereign's enemies....
Mock not my senseless conjuration, lords,
This earth shall have a feeling, and these stones
Prove arméd soldiers, ere her native king
Shall falter under foul rebellion's arms.   [*he rises*

  Carlisle. Fear not, my lord. That Power that made
    you king,
Hath power to keep you king in spite of all.
The means that heaven yields must be embraced,
30 And not neglected; else, if heaven would,
And we will not, heaven's offer we refuse,
The proffered means of succour and redress.

  Aumerle. He means, my lord, that we are too remiss,
Whilst Bolingbroke, through our security,
Grows strong and great in substance and in power.

  K. Richard. Discomfortable cousin! know'st thou not
That when the searching eye of heaven is hid,
Behind the globe, that lights the lower world,
Then thieves and robbers range abroad unseen,
40 In murders and in outrage, boldly here,
But when from under this terrestrial ball
He fires the proud tops of the eastern pines,
And darts his light through every guilty hole,
Then murders, treasons, and detested sins,
The cloak of night being plucked from off their backs,
Stand bare and naked, trembling at themselves?
So when this thief, this traitor, Bolingbroke,
Who all this while hath revelled in the night,
Whilst we were wand'ring with the antipodes,
50 Shall see us rising in our throne the east,
His treasons will sit blushing in his face,
Not able to endure the sight of day,
But self-affrighted tremble at his sin.
Not all the water in the rough rude sea

Can wash the balm off from an anointed king.
The breath of worldly men cannot depose
The deputy elected by the Lord,
For every man that Bolingbroke hath pressed
To lift shrewd steel against our golden crown,
God for his Richard hath in heavenly pay   60
A glorious angel; then, if angels fight,
Weak men must fall, for heaven still guards the right.

SALISBURY comes up

Welcome, my lord: how far off lies your power?
  Salisbury. Nor near nor farther off, my gracious lord,
Than this weak arm; discomfort guides my tongue,
And bids me speak of nothing but despair.
One day too late, I fear me, noble lord,
Hath clouded all thy happy days on earth:
O, call back yesterday, bid time return,
And thou shalt have twelve thousand fighting men!   70
To-day, to-day, unhappy day too late,
O'erthrows thy joys, friends, fortune and thy state,
For all the Welshmen, hearing thou wert dead,
Are gone to Bolingbroke, dispersed and fled.
  Aumerle. Comfort, my liege, why looks your grace
    so pale?
  K. Richard. But now the blood of twenty
    thousand men
Did triumph in my face, and they are fled:
And till so much blood thither come again,
  Have I not reason to look pale and dead?
All souls that will be safe, fly from my side,   80
For time hath set a blot upon my pride.
  Aumerle. Comfort, my liege, remember who you are.
  K. Richard. I had forgot myself, am I not king?
Awake thou coward majesty! thou sleepest.

Is not the king's name twenty thousand names?
Arm, arm, my name! a puny subject strikes
At thy great glory. Look not to the ground,
Ye favourites of a king, are we not high?
High be our thoughts. I know my uncle York
90 Hath power enough to serve our turn: but who
    comes here?

Scroop is seen approaching

   Scroop. More health and happiness betide my liege
Than can my care-tuned tongue deliver him.
   K. Richard. Mine ear is open, and my heart prepared,
The worst is worldly loss thou canst unfold.
Say, is my kingdom lost? why, 'twas my care,
And what loss is it to be rid of care?
Strives Bolingbroke to be as great as we?
Greater he shall not be. If he serve God,
We'll serve him too, and be his fellow so:
100 Revolt our subjects? that we cannot mend,
They break their faith to God as well as us:
Cry, woe, destruction, ruin, and decay,
The worst is death, and death will have his day.
   Scroop. Glad am I, that your highness is so armed
To bear the tidings of calamity.
Like an unseasonable stormy day,
Which makes the silver rivers drown their shores,
As if the world were all dissolved to tears;
So high above his limits swells the rage
110 Of Bolingbroke, covering your fearful land
With hard bright steel, and hearts harder than steel.
White-beards have armed their thin and hairless scalps
Against thy majesty: boys, with women's voices,
Strive to speak big and clap their female joints
In stiff unwieldy arms against thy crown,

Thy very beadsmen learn to bend their bows
Of double-fatal yew against thy state,
Yea, distaff-women manage rusty bills
Against thy seat. Both young and old rebel,
And all goes worse than I have power to tell.   120
  K. Richard. Too well, too well thou tell'st a tale so ill.
Where is the Earl of Wiltshire? where is Bagot?
What is become of Bushy? where is Green?
That they have let the dangerous enemy
Measure our confines with such peaceful steps?
If we prevail, their heads shall pay for it:
I warrant they have made peace with Bolingbroke.
  Scroop. Peace have they made with him, indeed,
        my lord.
  K. Richard. O villains, vipers, damned
        without redemption!
Dogs, easily won to fawn on any man!   130
Snakes, in my heart-blood warmed, that sting my heart!
Three Judases, each one thrice worse than Judas!
Would they make peace? terrible hell
Make war upon their spotted souls for this!
  Scroop. Sweet love, I see, changing his property,
Turns to the sourest and most deadly hate.
Again uncurse their souls, their peace is made
With heads and not with hands, those whom you curse
Have felt the worst of death's destroying wound,
And lie full low graved in the hollow ground.   140
  Aumerle. Is Bushy, Green, and the Earl of
        Wiltshire dead?
  Scroop. Ay, all of them at Bristow lost their heads.
  Aumerle. Where is the duke my father with his power?
  K. Richard. No matter where, of comfort no
        man speak:
Let's talk of graves, of worms, and epitaphs,

Make dust our paper, and with rainy eyes
Write sorrow on the bosom of the earth....
Let's choose executors and talk of wills:
And yet not so, for what can we bequeath,
150 Save our deposéd bodies to the ground?
Our lands, our lives, and all are Bolingbroke's,
And nothing can we call our own, but death;
And that small model of the barren earth,
Which serves as paste and cover to our bones.
For God's sake let us sit upon the ground,
And tell sad stories of the death of kings—
How some have been deposed, some slain in war,
Some haunted by the ghosts they have deposed,
Some poisoned by their wives, some sleeping killed;
160 All murdered—for within the hollow crown
That rounds the mortal temples of a king,
Keeps Death his court, and there the antic sits,
Scoffing his state and grinning at his pomp,
Allowing him a breath, a little scene,
To monarchize, be feared, and kill with looks,
Infusing him with self and vain conceit,
As if this flesh which walls about our life,
Were brass impregnable: and humoured thus,
Comes at the last, and with a little pin
170 Bores through his castle wall, and farewell king!
Cover your heads, and mock not flesh and blood
With solemn reverence, throw away respect,
Tradition, form, and ceremonious duty,
For you have but mistook me all this while:
I live with bread like you, feel want,
Taste grief, need friends—subjected thus,
How can you say to me, I am a king?
  Carlisle. My lord, wise men ne'er sit and wail
        their woes,

But presently prevent the ways to wail.
To fear the foe, since fear oppresseth strength,   180
Gives in your weakness strength unto your foe,
And so your follies fight against yourself:
Fear and be slain, no worse can come to fight,
And fight and die is death destroying death,
Where fearing dying pays death servile breath.
　Aumerle. My father hath a power, inquire of him,
And learn to make a body of a limb.
　K. Richard. Thou chid'st me well—proud
　　Bolingbroke, I come
To change blows with thee for our day of doom:
This ague fit of fear is over-blown.   190
An easy task it is to win our own....
Say, Scroop, where lies our uncle with his power?
Speak sweetly, man, although thy looks be sour.
　Scroop. Men judge by the complexion of the sky
　The state and inclination of the day;
So may you by my dull and heavy eye,
　My tongue hath but a heavier tale to say.
I play the torturer by small and small
To lengthen out the worst that must be spoken:
Your uncle York is joined with Bolingbroke,   200
And all your northern castles yielded up,
And all your southern gentlemen in arms
Upon his party.
　K. Richard.　　Thou hast said enough:
　　　　　　　　　　　　　　　　　[to Aumerle
Beshrew thee, cousin, which didst lead me forth
Of that sweet way I was in to despair!
What say you now? what comfort have we now?
By heaven I'll hate him everlastingly
That bids me be of comfort any more....
Go to Flint castle, there I'll pine away—

210 A king, woe's slave, shall kingly woe obey:
That power I have, discharge, and let them go
To ear the land that hath some hope to grow,
For I have none. Let no man speak again,
To alter this, for counsel is but vain.
        Aumerle. My liege, one word.
        K. Richard.   He does me double wrong,
That wounds me with the flatteries of his tongue....
Discharge my followers, let them hence away,
From Richard's night, to Bolingbroke's fair day.

                                        [*they go*

[3. 3.]   *Wales. Before Flint Castle*

Enter marching with drum and colours, BOLINGBROKE,
    YORK, NORTHUMBERLAND, *and their forces*

        Bolingbroke. So that by this intelligence we learn
The Welshmen are dispersed, and Salisbury
Is gone to meet the king, who lately landed
With some few private friends upon this coast.
        Northumberland. The news is very fair and good,
                my lord,
Richard, not far from hence, hath hid his head.
        York. It would beseem the Lord Northumberland,
To say 'King Richard': alack the heavy day,
When such a sacred king should hide his head.
10   *Northumberland.* Your grace mistakes; only to be brief
Left I his title out.
        York.   The time hath been,
Would you have been so brief with him, he would
Have been so brief with you, to shorten you,
For taking so the head, your whole head's length.
        Bolingbroke. Mistake not, uncle, further than
                you should.

York. Take not, good cousin, further than you should,
Lest you mis-take: the heavens are o'er our heads.

Bolingbroke. I know it, uncle, and oppose not myself
Against their will....But who comes here?

Enter PERCY

Welcome, Harry; what, will not this castle yield?   20
    Percy. The castle royally is manned, my lord,
Against thy entrance.
    Bolingbroke. Royally!
Why, it contains no king?
    Percy.   Yes, my good lord,
It doth contain a king. King Richard lies
Within the limits of yon lime and stone,
And with him are the Lord Aumerle, Lord Salisbury,
Sir Stephen Scroop, besides a clergyman
Of holy reverence, who I cannot learn.
    Northumberland. O belike it is the Bishop of Carlisle. 30
    Bolingbroke. Noble lord,   [*to Northumberland*
Go to the rude ribs of that ancient castle,
Through brazen trumpet send the breath of parley
Into his ruined ears, and thus deliver....
Henry Bolingbroke
On both his knees doth kiss King Richard's hand,
And sends allegiance and true faith of heart
To his most royal person: hither come
Even at his feet to lay my arms and power;
Provided that my banishment repealed   40
And lands restored again be freely granted;
If not, I'll use the advantage of my power,
And lay the summer's dust with showers of blood,
Rained from the wounds of slaughtered Englishmen,
The which, how far off from the mind of Bolingbroke
It is such crimson tempest should bedrench

The fresh green lap of fair King Richard's land,
My stooping duty tenderly shall show:
Go, signify as much, while here we march
50 Upon the grassy carpet of this plain...

[*Northumberland advances to the castle, with a trumpeter*

Let's march without the noise of threat'ning drum,
That from this castle's tattered battlements
Our fair appointments may be well perused....
Methinks, King Richard and myself should meet
With no less terror than the elements
Of fire and water, when their thund'ring shock
At meeting tears the cloudy cheeks of heaven.
Be he the fire, I'll be the yielding water;
The rage be his, whilst on the earth I rain
60 My waters—on the earth, and not on him....
March on, and mark King Richard how he looks.

*NORTHUMBERLAND sounds a parle without, and is answered
by another trumpet within: then a flourish. Enter on the
walls KING RICHARD, the BISHOP OF CARLISLE,
AUMERLE, SCROOP, and SALISBURY*

See, see, King Richard doth himself appear,
As doth the blushing discontented sun
From out the fiery portal of the east,
When he perceives the envious clouds are bent
To dim his glory, and to stain the track
Of his bright passage to the occident.
   York. Yet looks he like a king! behold his eye,
As bright as is the eagle's, lightens forth
70 Controlling majesty; alack, alack, for woe,
That any harm should stain so fair a show!
   K. Richard [*to Northumberland*]. We are amazed, and
      thus long have we stood
To watch the fearful bending of thy knee,

Because we thought ourself thy lawful king:
And if we be, how dare thy joints forget
To pay their awful duty to our presence?
If we be not, show us the hand of God
That hath dismissed us from our stewardship,
For well we know no hand of blood and bone
Can gripe the sacred handle of our sceptre,   80
Unless he do profane, steal, or usurp.
And though you think that all, as you have done,
Have torn their souls, by turning them from us,
And we are barren and bereft of friends...
Yet know, my master, God omnipotent,
Is mustering in his clouds, on our behalf,
Armies of pestilence, and they shall strike
Your children yet unborn, and unbegot,
That lift your vassal hands against my head,
And threat the glory of my precious crown....   90
Tell Bolingbroke—for yon methinks he stands—
That every stride he makes upon my land,
Is dangerous treason: he is come to open
The purple testament of bleeding war:
But ere the crown he looks for live in peace,
Ten thousand bloody crowns of mothers' sons
Shall ill become the flower of England's face,
Change the complexion of her maid-pale peace
To scarlet indignation and bedew
Her pasture's grass with faithful English blood.   100
  Northumberland. The king of heaven forbid our lord
      the king
Should so with civil and uncivil arms
Be rushed upon! Thy thrice noble cousin,
Harry Bolingbroke, doth humbly kiss thy hand,
And by the honourable tomb he swears,
That stands upon your royal grandsire's bones,

And by the royalties of both your bloods,
Currents that spring from one most gracious head,
And by the buried hand of warlike Gaunt,
110 And by the worth and honour of himself,
Comprising all that may be sworn or said,
His coming hither hath no further scope
Than for his lineal royalties, and to beg
Enfranchisement immediate on his knees,
Which on thy royal party granted once,
His glittering arms he will commend to rust,
His barbéd steeds to stables, and his heart
To faithful service of your majesty....
This swears he, as he is a prince, is just;
120 And, as I am a gentleman, I credit him.
 K. Richard. Northumberland, say thus the
   king returns—
His noble cousin is right welcome hither,
And all the number of his fair demands
Shall be accomplished without contradiction.
With all the gracious utterance thou hast,
Speak to his gentle hearing kind commends....
     [Northumberland retires to Bolingbroke,
       Richard turns to Aumerle
We do debase ourselves, cousin, do we not,
To look so poorly, and to speak so fair?
Shall we call back Northumberland and send
130 Defiance to the traitor, and so die?
 Aumerle. No, good my lord; let's fight with
   gentle words,
Till time lend friends, and friends their helpful swords.
 K. Richard. O God! O God! that e'er this tongue
   of mine,
That laid the sentence of dread banishment
On yon proud man, should take it off again

With words of sooth! O, that I were as great
As is my grief, or lesser than my name!
Or that I could forget what I have been!
Or not remember what I must be now!
Swell'st thou, proud heart? I'll give thee scope to beat,   140
Since foes have scope to beat both thee and me.

    Aumerle. Northumberland comes back
      from Bolingbroke.

   K. Richard. What must the king do now? must
      he submit?
The king shall do it: must he be deposed?
The king shall be contented: must he lose
The name of king? a God's name let it go:
I'll give my jewels for a set of beads:
My gorgeous palace for a hermitage:
My gay apparel for an almsman's gown:
My figured goblets for a dish of wood: 150
My sceptre for a palmer's walking-staff:
My subjects for a pair of carvéd saints,
And my large kingdom for a little grave,
A little little grave, an obscure grave,
Or I'll be buried in the king's highway,
Some way of common trade, where subjects' feet
May hourly trample on their sovereign's head;
For on my heart they tread now whilst I live:
And buried once, why not upon my head?
Aumerle, thou weep'st (my tender-hearted cousin!),   160
We'll make foul weather with despiséd tears;
Our sighs and they shall lodge the summer corn,
And make a dearth in this revolting land:
Or shall we play the wantons with our woes,
And make some pretty match with shedding tears?
As thus to drop them still upon one place,
Till they have fretted us a pair of graves

Within the earth, and therein laid...there lies
Two kinsmen digged their graves with weeping eyes!
170 Would not this ill do well? Well, well, I see
I talk but idly, and you laugh at me....
Most mighty prince, my Lord Northumberland,
What says King Bolingbroke? will his majesty
Give Richard leave to live till Richard die?
You make a leg, and Bolingbroke says 'ay'.
    Northumberland. My lord, in the base court he
        doth attend,
To speak with you, may it please you to come down?
    K. Richard. Down, down I come, like
        glist'ring Phaethon:
Wanting the manage of unruly jades....
180 In the base court? Base court, where kings grow base,
To come at traitors' calls, and do them grace.
In the base court? Come down? Down court!
        down king!
For night-owls shriek where mounting larks should sing.
                    [*he goes down from the battlements*
    Bolingbroke. [*coming forward*] What says his majesty?
    Northumberland.   Sorrow and grief of heart
Makes him speak fondly like a frantic man,
Yet he is come.

        KING RICHARD, *the* DUKE OF YORK *and*
                attendants come forth

    Bolingbroke. Stand all apart,
And show fair duty to his majesty...
My gracious lord.   [*'he kneels down'*
190   *K. Richard.* Fair cousin, you debase your
        princely knee,
To make the base earth proud with kissing it:
Me rather had my heart might feel your love,

Than my unpleased eye see your courtesy:
Up, cousin, up—your heart is up, I know,
Thus high [*touching his own head*] at least, although your
    knee be low.
  Bolingbroke. My gracious lord, I come but for
    mine own.
  K. Richard. Your own is yours, and I am yours
    and all.
  Bolingbroke. So far be mine, my most redoubted lord,
As my true service shall deserve your love.
  K. Richard. Well you deserve: they well deserve
    to have,   200
That know the strong'st and surest way to get.
Uncle, give me your hands, nay, dry your eyes,
Tears show their love, but want their remedies....
Cousin, I am too young to be your father,
Though you are old enough to be my heir.
What you will have, I'll give, and willing too,
For do we must, what force will have us do...
Set on towards London, cousin, is it so?
  Bolingbroke. Yea, my good lord.
  K. Richard.   Then I must not say no.
                                 [*they go*

[3. 4.]   *The* DUKE OF YORK'S *garden*

Enter the QUEEN *and two Ladies*

  Queen. What sport shall we devise here in this garden,
To drive away the heavy thought of care?
  Lady. Madam, we'll play at bowls.
  Queen. 'Twill make me think the world is full
    of rubs,

And that my fortune runs against the bias.

Lady. Madam, we'll dance.

Queen. My legs can keep no measure in delight,
When my poor heart no measure keeps in grief:
Therefore, no dancing, girl—some other sport.

10 *Lady.* Madam, we'll tell tales.

Queen. Of sorrow or of joy?

Lady.   Of either, madam.

Queen. Of neither, girl:
For if of joy, being altogether wanting,
It doth remember me the more of sorrow;
Or if of grief, being altogether had,
It adds more sorrow to my want of joy:
For what I have I need not to repeat,
And what I want it boots not to complain.

Lady. Madam, I'll sing.

Queen.   'Tis well that thou hast cause,
20 But thou shouldst please me better, wouldst thou weep.

Lady. I could weep, madam, would it do you good.

Queen. And I could sing, would weeping do
        me good,
And never borrow any tear of thee....

'Enter Gardeners' with spades &c.

But stay, here come the gardeners.
Let's step into the shadow of these trees.
My wretchedness unto a row of pins,
They will talk of state, for every one doth so
Against a change: woe is forerun with woe.

[*Queen and her ladies retire*

Gardener. [*to one of his men*] Go, bind thou up yon
        dangling apricocks,

30 Which like unruly children make their sire

Stoop with oppression of their prodigal weight,
Give some supportance to the bending twigs.
[to the other] Go thou, and like an executioner
Cut off the heads of too fast growing sprays,
That look too lofty in our commonwealth—
All must be even in our government....
You thus employed, I will go root away
The noisome weeds which without profit suck
The soil's fertility from wholesome flowers.

   Man. Why should we, in the compass of a pale,   40
Keep law and form and due proportion,
Showing as in a model our firm estate,
When our sea-wallèd garden, the whole land,
Is full of weeds, her fairest flowers choked up,
Her fruit-trees all unpruned, her hedges ruined,
Her knots disordered, and her wholesome herbs
Swarming with caterpillars?

   Gardener.   Hold thy peace—
He that hath suffered this disordered spring
Hath now himself met with the fall of leaf:
The weeds which his broad-spreading leaves   50
     did shelter,
That seemed in eating him to hold him up,
Are plucked up root and all by Bolingbroke—
I mean the Earl of Wiltshire, Bushy, Green.

   Man. What, are they dead?

   Gardener.   They are, and Bolingbroke
Hath seized the wasteful king. O! what pity is it
That he had not so trimmed and dressed his land,
As we this garden! We at time of year
Do wound the bark, the skin of our fruit-trees,
Lest being over-proud in sap and blood,
With too much riches it confound itself.   60
Had he done so to great and growing men,

They might have lived to bear, and he to taste,
Their fruits of duty: superfluous branches
We lop away, that bearing boughs may live:
Had he done so, himself had borne the crown,
Which waste of idle hours hath quite thrown down.
Man. What, think you then the king shall be deposed?
Gardener. Depressed he is already, and deposed
'Tis doubt he will be....Letters came last night
70 To a dear friend of the good Duke of York's,
That tell black tidings.
　　Queen. O, I am pressed to death through want
　　　　of speaking!　　　　　　　　　　　　　*[comes forth*
Thou, old Adam's likeness, set to dress this garden,
How dares thy harsh rude tongue sound this
　　　　unpleasing news?
What Eve, what serpent, hath suggested thee
To make a second fall of cursèd man?
Why dost thou say King Richard is deposed?
Dar'st thou, thou little better thing than earth,
Divine his downfal? Say, where, when, and how,
80 Cam'st thou by these ill tidings? speak, thou wretch!
　　Gardener. Pardon me, madam. Little joy have I
To breathe this news, yet what I say is true:
King Richard, he is in the mighty hold
Of Bolingbroke: their fortunes both are weighed:
In your lord's scale is nothing but himself,
And some few vanities that make him light;
But in the balance of great Bolingbroke,
Besides himself, are all the English peers,
And with that odds he weighs King Richard down;
90 Post you to London, and you will find it so,
I speak no more than every one doth know.
　　Queen. Nimble mischance, that art so light
　　　　of foot,

Doth not thy embassage belong to me,
And am I last that knows it? O, thou thinkest
To serve me last, that I may longest keep
Thy sorrow in my breast...Come, ladies, go,
To meet at London London's king in woe....
What, was I born to this, that my sad look
Should grace the triumph of great Bolingbroke?
Gardener, for telling me these news of woe,   100
Pray God the plants thou graft'st may never grow.
                    [*she leaves the garden with her ladies*

Gardener. Poor queen! so that thy state might be
    no worse,
I would my skill were subject to thy curse:
Here did she fall a tear, here in this place
I'll set a bank of rue, sour herb of grace.
Rue, even for ruth, here shortly shall be seen,
In the remembrance of a weeping queen.   [*they go*

[4. 1.]   *Westminster Hall, with
                    the king's throne*

Enter as to the Parliament BOLINGBROKE, AUMERLE,
SURREY, NORTHUMBERLAND, PERCY, FITZWATER, *and
other lords, the* BISHOP OF CARLISLE, *and the* ABBOT OF
WESTMINSTER. *Herald and Officers with* BAGOT

Bolingbroke. Call forth Bagot....
                    [*he is brought forward*
Now, Bagot, freely speak thy mind,
What thou dost know of noble Gloucester's death,
Who wrought it with the king, and who performed
The bloody office of his timeless end.
Bagot. Then set before my face the Lord Aumerle.

Bolingbroke. Cousin, stand forth, and look upon
      that man.

  Bagot. My Lord Aumerle, I know your daring tongue
Scorns to unsay what once it hath delivered.
10 In that dead time when Gloucester's death was plotted,
I heard you say, 'Is not my arm of length,
That reacheth from the restful English court
As far as Calais, to my uncle's head?'
Amongst much other talk that very time
I heard you say that you had rather refuse
The offer of an hundred thousand crowns
Than Bolingbroke's return to England—
Adding withal, how blest this land would be,
In this your cousin's death.

  Aumerle.   Princes and noble lords,
20 What answer shall I make to this base man?
Shall I so much dishonour my fair stars,
On equal terms to give him chastisement?
Either I must, or have mine honour soiled
With the attainder of his slanderous lips.
There is my gage, the manual seal of death,
That marks thee out for hell! I say thou liest,
And will maintain what thou hast said is false
In thy heart-blood, though being all too base
To stain the temper of my knightly sword.
30 *Bolingbroke.* Bagot, forbear, thou shalt not take it up.
  Aumerle. Excepting one, I would he were the best
In all this presence that hath moved me so.

  Fitzwater. If that thy valour stand on sympathy,
There is my gage, Aumerle, in gage to thine:
By that fair sun which shows me where thou stand'st,
I heard thee say, and vauntingly thou spak'st it,
That thou wert cause of noble Gloucester's death.
If thou deny'st it twenty times, thou liest,

And I will turn thy falsehood to thy heart,
Where it was forgéd, with my rapier's point.   40
  Aumerle. Thou dar'st not, coward, live to see that day.
  Fitzwater. Now, by my soul, I would it were this hour.
  Aumerle. Fitzwater, thou art damned to hell for this.
  Percy. Aumerle, thou liest, his honour is as true
In this appeal as thou art all unjust,
And that thou art so, there I throw my gage,
To prove it on thee to the extremest point
Of mortal breathing—seize it if thou dar'st.
  Aumerle. An if I do not, may my hands rot off,
And never brandish more revengeful steel   50
Over the glittering helmet of my foe!
  Another Lord. I task the earth to the like,
    forsworn Aumerle,
And spur thee on with full as many lies
As may be holloaed in thy treacherous ear
From sun to sun: there is my honour's pawn—
Engage it to the trial if thou darest.
  Aumerle. Who sets me else? by heaven, I'll throw
    at all!
I have a thousand spirits in one breast,
To answer twenty thousand such as you.
  Surrey. My Lord Fitzwater, I do remember well   60
The very time Aumerle and you did talk.
  Fitzwater. 'Tis very true, you were in presence then,
And you can witness with me this is true.
  Surrey. As false, by heaven, as heaven itself is true.
  Fitzwater. Surrey, thou liest.
  Surrey.   Dishonourable boy!
That lie shall lie so heavy on my sword,
That it shall render vengeance and revenge,
Till thou the lie-giver, and that lie, do lie
In earth as quiet as thy father's skull....

70 In proof whereof, there is my honour's pawn—
Engage it to the trial if thou dar'st.
 Fitzwater. How fondly dost thou spur a
  forward horse!
If I dare eat, or drink, or breathe, or live,
I dare meet Surrey in a wilderness,
And spit upon him, whilst I say he lies,
And lies, and lies: there is my bond of faith,
To tie thee to my strong correction:
As I intend to thrive in this new world,
Aumerle is guilty of my true appeal:
80 Besides, I heard the banished Norfolk say,
That thou, Aumerle, didst send two of thy men
To execute the noble duke at Calais.
 Aumerle. Some honest Christian trust me with a gage,
That Norfolk lies—here do I throw down this,
If he may be repealed to try his honour.
 Bolingbroke. These differences shall all rest under gage,
Till Norfolk be repealed. Repealed he shall be,
And, though mine enemy, restored again
To all his lands and signories: when he's returned,
90 Against Aumerle we will enforce his trial.
 Carlisle. That honourable day shall ne'er be seen.
Many a time hath banished Norfolk fought
For Jesu Christ in glorious Christian field,
Streaming the ensign of the Christian cross
Against black pagans, Turks, and Saracens,
And toiled with works of war, retired himself
To Italy, and there at Venice gave
His body to that pleasant country's earth,
And his pure soul unto his captain Christ
100 Under whose colours he had fought so long.
 Bolingbroke. Why, bishop, is Norfolk dead?
 Carlisle. As surely as I live, my lord.

Bolingbroke. Sweet peace conduct his sweet soul to
    the bosom
Of good old Abraham! Lords appellants,
Your differences shall all rest under gage,
Till we assign you to your days of trial.

YORK enters the hall

York. Great Duke of Lancaster, I come to thee
From plume-plucked Richard, who with willing soul
Adopts thee heir, and his high sceptre yields
To the possession of thy royal hand: 110
Ascend his throne, descending now from him,
And long live Henry, of that name the fourth!
  Bolingbroke. In God's name, I'll ascend the
    regal throne.
  Carlisle. Marry, God forbid!
Worst in this royal presence may I speak,
Yet best beseeming me to speak the truth.
Would God that any in this noble presence
Were enough noble to be upright judge
Of noble Richard....Then true noblesse would
Learn him forbearance from so foul a wrong.   120
What subject can give sentence on his king?
And who sits here that is not Richard's subject?
Thieves are not judged but they are by to hear,
Although apparent guilt be seen in them,
And shall the figure of God's majesty,
His captain, steward, deputy-elect,
Anointed, crowned, planted many years,
Be judged by subject and inferior breath,
And he himself not present? O, forfend it, God,
That in a Christian climate souls refined   130
Should show so heinous, black, obscene a deed!
I speak to subjects, and a subject speaks,

Stirred up by God thus boldly for his king.
My Lord of Hereford here, whom you call king,
Is a foul traitor to proud Hereford's king,
And if you crown him, let me prophesy,
The blood of English shall manure the ground,
And future ages groan for this foul act,
Peace shall go sleep with Turks and infidels,
140 And, in this seat of peace, tumultuous wars
Shall kin with kin, and kind with kind confound;
Disorder, horror, fear, and mutiny
Shall here inhabit, and this land be called
The field of Golgotha and dead men's skulls.
O, if you raise this house against this house,
It will the woefullest division prove
That ever fell upon this cursèd earth:
Prevent 't, resist it, let it not be so,
Lest child, child's children, cry against you 'woe!'
150 *Northumberland.* Well have you argued, sir, and, for
　　　your pains,
Of capital treason we arrest you here:
My Lord of Westminster, be it your charge
To keep him safely till his day of trial....
May it please you, lords, to grant the commons' suit?
　Bolingbroke. Fetch hither Richard, that in
　　　common view
He may surrender; so we shall proceed
Without suspicion.
　York.　　　　　I will be his conduct.　　*[he goes*
　Bolingbroke. Lords, you that here are under
　　　our arrest,
Procure your sureties for your days of answer:
160 Little are we beholding to your love,
And little looked for at your helping hands.

*YORK returns with KING RICHARD, guarded and stripped
of his royal robes; Officers follow bearing the Crown, &c.*

K. Richard. Alack, why am I sent for to a king,
Before I have shook off the regal thoughts
Wherewith I reigned? I hardly yet have learned
To insinuate, flatter, bow, and bend my knee:
Give sorrow leave awhile to tutor me
To this submission....Yet I well remember
The favours of these men: were they not mine?
Did they not sometime cry 'all hail!' to me?
So Judas did to Christ: but he, in twelve,　　　170
Found truth in all, but one; I, in twelve thousand, none....
God save the king! Will no man say amen?
Am I both priest and clerk? well then, amen.
God save the king! although I be not he;
And yet, amen, if heaven do think him me....
To do what service am I sent for hither?
　York. To do that office of thine own good will,
Which tired majesty did make thee offer:
The resignation of thy state and crown
To Henry Bolingbroke.　　　180
　K. Richard. Give me the crown....Here, cousin, seize
　　the crown:
Here, cousin,
On this side, my hand, and on that side, thine....
Now is this golden crown like a deep well
That owes two buckets, filling one another,
The emptier ever dancing in the air,
The other down, unseen, and full of water:
That bucket down, and full of tears, am I,
Drinking my griefs, whilst you mount up on high.
　Bolingbroke. I thought you had been willing to resign. 190

K. Richard. My crown I am, but still my griefs
    are mine:
You may my glories and my state depose,
But not my griefs; still am I king of those.
  Bolingbroke. Part of your cares you give me with
    your crown.
  K. Richard. Your cares set up do not pluck my
    cares down.
My care is loss of care, by old care done,
Your care is gain of care, by new care won:
The cares I give, I have, though given away,
They tend the crown, yet still with me they stay.
200 *Bolingbroke.* Are you contented to resign the crown?
  K. Richard. Ay, no; no, ay; for I must nothing be:
Therefore no 'no', for I resign to thee....
Now mark me how I will undo myself:
I give this heavy weight from off my head,
And this unwieldy sceptre from my hand,
The pride of kingly sway from out my heart;
With mine own tears I wash away my balm,
With mine own hands I give away my crown,
With mine own tongue deny my sacred state,
210 With mine own breath release all duteous oaths:
All pomp and majesty I do forswear;
My manors, rents, revenues, I forgo;
My acts, decrees, and statutes, I deny:
God pardon all oaths that are broke to me!
God keep all vows unbroke are made to thee!
Make me, that nothing have, with nothing grieved,
And thou with all pleased, that hast all achieved!
Long mayst thou live in Richard's seat to sit,
And soon lie Richard in an earthy pit....
220 God save King Henry, unkinged Richard says,
And send him many years of sunshine days....

What more remains?

Northumberland.   No more, but that you read
These accusations and these grievous crimes,
Committed by your person and your followers
Against the state and profit of this land;
That, by confessing them, the souls of men
May deem that you are worthily deposed.

K. Richard. Must I do so? and must I ravel out
My weaved-up follies? Gentle Northumberland,
If thy offences were upon record,   230
Would it not shame thee, in so fair a troop,
To read a lecture of them? If thou wouldst,
There shouldst thou find one heinous article,
Containing the deposing of a king,
And cracking the strong warrant of an oath,
Marked with a blot, damned in the book of heaven....
Nay, all of you, that stand and look upon me,
Whilst that my wretchedness doth bait myself,
Though some of you, with Pilate, wash your hands,
Showing an outward pity; yet you Pilates   240
Have here delivered me to my sour cross,
And water cannot wash away your sin.

Northumberland. My lord, dispatch, read o'er
    these articles.

K. Richard. Mine eyes are full of tears, I cannot see:
And yet salt water blinds them not so much,
But they can see a sort of traitors here.
Nay, if I turn mine eyes upon myself,
I find myself a traitor with the rest:
For I have given here my soul's consent
T' undeck the pompous body of a king;   250
Made glory base; and sovereignty, a slave;
Proud majesty, a subject; state, a peasant.

Northumberland. My lord—

K. Richard. No lord of thine, thou haught,
              insulting man;
Nor no man's lord; I have no name, no title;
No, not that name was given me at the font,
But 'tis usurped: alack the heavy day,
That I have worn so many winters out,
And know not now what name to call myself!
260 O, that I were a mockery king of snow,
Standing before the sun of Bolingbroke,
To melt myself away in water-drops!
Good king, great king, and yet not greatly good,
An if my word be sterling yet in England,
Let it command a mirror hither straight,
That it may show me what a face I have,
Since it is bankrupt of his majesty.
      Bolingbroke. Go some of you, and fetch a looking-glass.
                                    [*an attendant goes out*
      Northumberland. Read o'er this paper, while the glass
              doth come.
270 *K. Richard.* Fiend, thou torments me ere I come
              to hell.
      Bolingbroke. Urge it no more, my Lord
              Northumberland.
      Northumberland. The commons will not then
              be satisfied.
      K. Richard. They shall be satisfied; I'll read enough,
When I do see the very book indeed
Where all my sins are writ, and that's myself.

                The attendant returns with a glass

Give me that glass, and therein will I read....
No deeper wrinkles yet? hath sorrow struck
So many blows upon this face of mine,
And made no deeper wounds? O, flatt'ring glass,

Like to my followers in prosperity,   280
Thou dost beguile me! Was this face the face
That every day under his household roof
Did keep ten thousand men? Was this the face,
That, like the sun, did make beholders wink?
Was this the face, that faced so many follies,
And was at last out-faced by Bolingbroke?
A brittle glory shineth in this face,
As brittle as the glory is the face,
                    [*he dashes the glass to the ground*
For there it is, cracked in a hundred shivers....
Mark, silent king, the moral of this sport,   290
How soon my sorrow hath destroyed my face.
  Bolingbroke. The shadow of your sorrow
        hath destroyed
The shadow of your face.
  K. Richard.   Say that again.
The shadow of my sorrow...ha! let's see—
'Tis very true, my grief lies all within,
And these external manners of lament
Are merely shadows to the unseen grief,
That swells with silence in the tortured soul....
There lies the substance: and I thank thee, king,
For thy great bounty, that not only giv'st   300
Me cause to wail, but teachest me the way
How to lament the cause....I'll beg one boon,
And then be gone, and trouble you no more.
Shall I obtain it?
  Bolingbroke.   Name it, fair cousin.
  K. Richard. 'Fair cousin'? I am greater than a king:
For when I was a king, my flatterers
Were then but subjects; being now a subject,
I have a king here to my flatterer:
Being so great, I have no need to beg.

310 *Bolingbroke.* Yet ask.

 K. Richard. And shall I have?

 Bolingbroke. You shall.

 K. Richard. Then give me leave to go.

 Bolingbroke. Whither?

 K. Richard. Whither you will, so I were from
  your sights.

 Bolingbroke. Go, some of you, convey him to the Tower.

 K. Richard. O, good! convey? conveyers are you all,
That rise thus nimbly by a true king's fall.

 [*certain lords conduct Richard guarded from the hall*

 Bolingbroke. On Wednesday next we solemnly set down
320 Our coronation: lords, prepare yourselves.

*BOLINGBROKE and the Lords depart in procession: the
ABBOT OF WESTMINSTER, the BISHOP OF CARLISLE and
AUMERLE linger behind*

 Abbot. A woeful pageant have we here beheld.

 Carlisle. The woe's to come—the children yet unborn
Shall feel this day as sharp to them as thorn.

 Aumerle. You holy clergymen, is there no plot
To rid the realm of this pernicious blot?

 Abbot. My lord,
Before I freely speak my mind herein,
You shall not only take the sacrament
To bury mine intents, but also to effect
330 Whatever I shall happen to devise:
I see your brows are full of discontent,
Your hearts of sorrow, and your eyes of tears:
Come home with me to supper; I will lay
A plot shall show us all a merry day.   [*they go*

[5. 1.] *London. A street leading to the Tower*

'*Enter the* QUEEN *with her attendants*'

Queen. This way the king will come, this is the way
To Julius Cæsar's ill-erected tower,
To whose flint bosom my condemnéd lord
Is doomed a prisoner by proud Bolingbroke....
Here let us rest, if this rebellious earth
Have any resting for her true king's queen.

RICHARD *with guards comes into the street*

But soft, but see, or rather do not see,
My fair rose wither—yet look up, behold,
That you in pity may dissolve to dew,
And wash him fresh again with true-love tears...   10
Ah, thou, the model where old Troy did stand!
Thou map of honour, thou King Richard's tomb,
And not King Richard; thou most beauteous inn,
Why should hard-favoured grief be lodged in thee,
When triumph is become an alehouse guest?
  Richard. Join not with grief, fair woman, do not so,
To make my end too sudden. Learn, good soul,
To think our former state a happy dream,
From which awaked, the truth of what we are
Shows us but this: I am sworn brother, sweet,   20
To grim Necessity, and he and I
Will keep a league till death....Hie thee to France,
And cloister thee in some religious house.
Our holy lives must win a new world's crown,
Which our profane hours here have throwen down.
  Queen. What, is my Richard both in shape and mind
Transformed and weak'ned? hath Bolingbroke deposed
Thine intellect? hath he been in thy heart?

The lion dying thrusteth forth his paw,
30 And wounds the earth, if nothing else, with rage
To be o'erpowered, and wilt thou pupil-like
Take the correction, mildly kiss the rod,
And fawn on rage with base humility,
Which art a lion and the king of beasts?
    Richard. A king of beasts, indeed! if aught but beasts,
I had been still a happy king of men....
Good sometimes queen, prepare thee hence for France.
Think I am dead, and that even here thou takest
As from my death-bed thy last living leave;
40 In winter's tedious nights sit by the fire
With good old folks, and let them tell thee tales
Of woeful ages long ago betid;
And ere thou bid good night, to quit their griefs,
Tell thou the lamentable fall of me,
And send the hearers weeping to their beds:
For why, the senseless brands will sympathize
The heavy accent of thy moving tongue,
And in compassion weep the fire out,
And some will mourn in ashes, some coal-black,
50 For the deposing of a rightful king.

NORTHUMBERLAND *comes up*

    Northumberland. My lord, the mind of Bolingbroke
        is changed,
You must to Pomfret, not unto the Tower....
And, madam, there is order ta'en for you,
With all swift speed you must away to France.
    Richard. Northumberland, thou ladder wherewithal
The mounting Bolingbroke ascends my throne,
The time shall not be many hours of age
More than it is, ere foul sin gathering head
Shall break into corruption. Thou shalt think,

Though he divide the realm and give thee half,   60
It is too little, helping him to all....
And he shall think that thou, which knowest the way
To plant unrightful kings, wilt know again,
Being ne'er so little urged another way
To pluck him headlong from the usurped throne:
The love of wicked men converts to fear,
That fear to hate, and hate turns one or both
To worthy danger and deservéd death.
  Northumberland. My guilt be on my head, and there
    an end:
Take leave and part, for you must part forthwith.   70
  Richard. Doubly divorced! Bad men, you violate
A twofold marriage—'twixt my crown and me,
And then betwixt me and my married wife....
Let me unkiss the oath 'twixt thee and me;
And yet not so, for with a kiss 'twas made....
Part us, Northumberland—I towards the north,
Where shivering cold and sickness pines the clime;
My wife to France, from whence set forth in pomp
She came adornéd hither like sweet May,
Sent back like Hallowmas or short'st of day.   80
  Queen. And must we be divided? must we part?
  Richard. Ay, hand from hand, my love, and heart
    from heart.
  Queen. Banish us both, and send the king with me.
  Northumberland. That were some love, but
    little policy.
  Queen. Then whither he goes, thither let me go.
  Richard. So two, together weeping, make one woe.
Weep thou for me in France, I for thee here;
Better far off than near, be ne'er the near.
Go, count thy way with sighs, I mine with groans.
  Queen. So longest way shall have the longest moans.   90

Richard. Twice for one step I'll groan, the way
        being short,
And piece the way out with a heavy heart....
Come, come, in wooing sorrow let's be brief,
Since, wedding it, there is such length in grief:
One kiss shall stop our mouths, and dumbly part—
Thus give I mine, and thus take I thy heart. [*they kiss*
Queen. Give me mine own again, 'twere no good part
To take on me to keep and kill thy heart:
                                [*they kiss again*
So, now I have mine own again, be gone,
100 That I may strive to kill it with a groan.
Richard. We make woe wanton with this fond delay,
Once more, adieu, the rest let sorrow say.   [*they go*

[5. 2.]   *The Duke of York's palace*

The DUKE OF YORK *and the* DUCHESS

Duchess. My lord, you told me you would tell the rest,
When weeping made you break the story off
Of our two cousins coming into London.
York. Where did I leave?
Duchess.   At that sad stop, my lord,
Where rude misgoverned hands, from windows' tops,
Threw dust and rubbish on King Richard's head.
York. Then, as I said, the duke, great Bolingbroke,
Mounted upon a hot and fiery steed,
Which his aspiring rider seemed to know,
10 With slow but stately pace kept on his course,
Whilst all tongues cried 'God save thee, Bolingbroke!'
You would have thought the very windows spake,
So many greedy looks of young and old
Through casements darted their desiring eyes

Upon his visage, and that all the walls
With painted imagery had said at once
'Jesu preserve thee! welcome, Bolingbroke!'
Whilst he from one side to the other turning
Bareheaded, lower than his proud steed's neck,
Bespake them thus: 'I thank you, countrymen':   20
And thus still doing, thus he passed along.
  Duchess. Alack poor Richard! where rode he
    the whilst?
  York. As in a theatre the eyes of men,
After a well-graced actor leaves the stage,
Are idly bent on him that enters next,
Thinking his prattle to be tedious;
Even so, or with much more contempt, men's eyes
Did scowl on Richard; no man cried, 'God
    save him!'
No joyful tongue gave him his welcome home,
But dust was thrown upon his sacred head;   30
Which with such gentle sorrow he shook off,
His face still combating with tears and smiles,
The badges of his grief and patience,
That had not God for some strong purpose steeled
The hearts of men, they must perforce have melted,
And barbarism itself have pitied him:
But heaven hath a hand in these events,
To whose high will we bound our calm contents....
To Bolingbroke are we sworn subjects now,
Whose state and honour I for aye allow.   40

AUMERLE comes to the door

  Duchess. Here comes my son Aumerle.
  York.   Aumerle that was,
But that is lost for being Richard's friend:
And, madam, you must call him Rutland now:

I am in parliament pledge for his truth
And lasting fealty to the new made king.

   Duchess. Welcome, my son. Who are the violets now,
That strew the green lap of the new come spring?

   Aumerle. Madam, I know not, nor I greatly care not.
God knows I had as lief be none as one.

50 *York.* Well, bear you well in this new spring of time,
Lest you be cropped before you come to prime.
What news from Oxford? do these justs and
      triumphs hold?

   Aumerle. For aught I know, my lord, they do.

   York. You will be there, I know.

   Aumerle. If God prevent not, I purpose so.

   York. What seal is that, that hangs without thy bosom?
Yea, look'st thou pale? let me see the writing.

   Aumerle. My lord, 'tis nothing.

   York.   No matter then who see it.
I will be satisfied, let me see the writing.

60 *Aumerle.* I do beseech your grace to pardon me;
It is a matter of small consequence,
Which for some reasons I would not have seen.

   York. Which for some reasons, sir, I mean to see....
I fear, I fear—

   Duchess.   What should you fear?
'Tis nothing but some bond that he is ent'red into
For gay apparel 'gainst the triumph day.

   York. Bound to himself! what doth he with a bond,
That he is bound to? Wife, thou art a fool...
Boy, let me see the writing.

70 *Aumerle.* I do beseech you, pardon me, I may not
      show it.

   York. I will be satisfied, let me see it, I say.

              ['*he plucks it out of his bosom and reads it*'
Treason! foul treason! villain! traitor! slave!

Duchess. What is the matter, my lord?
York. [*shouts*] Ho! who is within there? saddle
　　my horse.　　　　　　　　　[*he reads again*
God for his mercy! what treachery is here!
Duchess. Why, what is it, my lord?
York. [*shouts louder*] Give me my boots I say, saddle
　　my horse.　　　　　　　　　[*he reads again*
Now by mine honour, by my life, by my troth,
I will appeach the villain.
　　Duchess.　　　　　　　What is the matter?
York. Peace, foolish woman.　　　　　　　　80
Duchess. I will not peace. What is the matter, Aumerle?
Aumerle. Good mother, be content—it is no more
Than my poor life must answer.
　　Duchess.　　　　　　　Thy life answer!
York. Bring me my boots, I will unto the king.

　　　'His man enters with his boots'

Duchess. Strike him, Aumerle. Poor boy, thou
　　art amazed.
Hence, villain! never more come in my sight.
York. [*to the man*] Give me my boots, I say.
　　　　　　　　[*the man helps him into them*
Duchess. Why, York, what wilt thou do?
Wilt thou not hide the trespass of thine own?
Have we more sons? or are we like to have?　　90
Is not my teeming date drunk up with time?
And wilt thou pluck my fair son from mine age,
And rob me of a happy mother's name?
Is he not like thee? is he not thine own?
York. Thou fond mad woman,
Wilt thou conceal this dark conspiracy?
A dozen of them here have ta'en the sacrament,
And interchangeably set down their hands,

To kill the king at Oxford.

   Duchess.   He shall be none.

100 We'll keep him here, then what is that to him?

   York. Away, fond woman! were he twenty times
       my son,
I would appeach him.

   Duchess.   Hadst thou groaned for him
As I have done, thou wouldst be more pitiful.
But now I know thy mind, thou dost suspect
That I have been disloyal to thy bed,
And that he is a bastard, not thy son:
Sweet York, sweet husband, be not of that mind,
He is as like thee as a man may be,
Not like to me, or any of my kin,
110 And yet I love him.

   York.   Make way, unruly woman.

                         [*he stalks forth*
   Duchess. After, Aumerle; mount thee upon his horse,
Spur post, and get before him to the king,
And beg thy pardon ere he do accuse thee.
I'll not be long behind—though I be old,
I doubt not but to ride as fast as York,
And never will I rise up from the ground,
Till Bolingbroke have pardoned thee: away, be gone!

                         [*they hurry out*

[5. 3.]   *Windsor Castle*

Enter BOLINGBROKE, PERCY *and other nobles*

   Bolingbroke. Can no man tell me of my unthrifty son?
'Tis full three months since I did see him last,
If any plague hang over us, 'tis he:
I would to God, my lords, he might be found:

Inquire at London, 'mongst the taverns there,
For there, they say, he daily doth frequent,
With unrestrainéd loose companions,
Even such, they say, as stand in narrow lanes,
And beat our watch, and rob our passengers,
While he, young wanton and effeminate boy,   10
Takes on the point of honour to support
So dissolute a crew.

Percy. My lord, some two days since I saw the prince,
And told him of those triumphs held at Oxford.

Bolingbroke. And what said the gallant?

Percy. His answer was, he would unto the stews,
And from the common'st creature pluck a glove,
And wear it as a favour, and with that
He would unhorse the lustiest challenger.

Bolingbroke. As dissolute as desperate—yet through both 20
I see some sparks of better hope, which elder years
May happily bring forth....But who comes here?

'Enter AUMERLE amazed'

Aumerle. Where is the king?

Bolingbroke. What means our cousin, that he stares
      and looks
So wildly?

Aumerle. God save your grace, I do beseech
      your majesty,
To have some conference with your grace alone.

Bolingbroke. Withdraw yourselves, and leave us
      here alone....   [*Percy and the rest withdraw*
What is the matter with our cousin now?

Aumerle. [*kneels*] For ever may my knees grow to
      the earth,   30
My tongue cleave to my roof within my mouth,
Unless a pardon ere I rise or speak.

Bolingbroke. Intended, or committed, was this fault?
If on the first, how heinous e'er it be,
To win thy after-love, I pardon thee.
  Aumerle. Then give me leave that I may turn the key,
That no man enter till my tale be done.
  Bolingbroke. Have thy desire.   [*the key is turned*

'*The* DUKE OF YORK *knocks at the door and crieth*'

  York. [*without*] My liege, beware, look to thyself,
40 Thou hast a traitor in thy presence there.
  Bolingbroke. Villain, I'll make thee safe.   [*he draws*
  Aumerle. [*kneels again*] Stay thy revengeful hand, thou
          hast no cause to fear.
  York. [*without*] Open the door, secure, foolhardy king,
Shall I for love speak treason to thy face?
Open the door, or I will break it open.

BOLINGBROKE *opens, admits* YORK *and locks
the door again*

  Bolingbroke. What is the matter, uncle? speak,
          recover breath,
Tell us how near is danger,
That we may arm us to encounter it.
  York. Peruse this writing here, and thou shalt know
                              [*he delivers the indenture*
50 The treason that my haste forbids me show.
  Aumerle. Remember, as thou read'st, thy
          promise passed.
I do repent me, read not my name there,
My heart is not confederate with my hand.
  York. It was, villain, ere thy hand did set it down....
I tore it from the traitor's bosom, king.
Fear, and not love, begets his penitence:

Forget to pity him, lest thy pity prove
A serpent that will sting thee to the heart.
 Bolingbroke. O heinous, strong, and bold conspiracy!
O loyal father of a treacherous son!   60
Thou sheer, immaculate and silver fountain,
From whence this stream, through muddy passages,
Hath held his current, and defiled himself!
Thy overflow of good converts to bad;
And thy abundant goodness shall excuse
This deadly blot in thy digressing son.
 York. So shall my virtue be his vice's bawd,
And he shall spend mine honour with his shame,
As thriftless sons their scraping fathers' gold:
Mine honour lives when his dishonour dies, 70
Or my shamed life in his dishonour lies.
Thou kill'st me in his life—giving him breath,
The traitor lives, the true man's put to death.
 Duchess. [*without*] What ho, my liege! for God's sake,
  let me in.
 Bolingbroke. What shrill-voiced suppliant makes this
  eager cry?
 Duchess. A woman, and thy aunt, great king—'tis I.
Speak with me, pity me, open the door,
A beggar begs that never begged before.
 Bolingbroke. Our scene is altered from a serious thing,
And now changed to 'The Beggar and the King': 80
My dangerous cousin, let your mother in,
I know she is come to pray for your foul sin.
 York. If thou do pardon, whosoever pray,
More sins for this forgiveness prosper may:
This fest'red joint cut off, the rest rest sound,
This let alone will all the rest confound.

Aumerle admits the Duchess

Duchess. O king, believe not this hard-hearted man!
Love loving not itself none other can.
  York. Thou frantic woman, what dost thou
      make here?
90 Shall thy old dugs once more a traitor rear?
  Duchess. Sweet York, be patient. Hear me,
      gentle liege.   [*she kneels*
  Bolingbroke. Rise up, good aunt.
  Duchess.   Not yet, I thee beseech.
For ever will I walk upon my knees,
And never see day that the happy sees,
Till thou give joy—until thou bid me joy,
By pardoning Rutland, my transgressing boy.
  Aumerle. Unto my mother's prayers I bend my knee.
                                       [*kneels*
  York. Against them both my true joints bended be.
                                       [*kneels*

Ill mayst thou thrive, if thou grant any grace!
100 *Duchess*. Pleads he in earnest? look upon his face;
His eyes do drop no tears, his prayers are in jest.
His words come from his mouth, ours from our breast.
He prays but faintly, and would be denied,
We pray with heart and soul, and all beside:
His weary joints would gladly rise, I know,
Our knees shall kneel till to the ground they grow.
His prayers are full of false hypocrisy,
Ours of true zeal and deep integrity.
Our prayers do out-pray his—then let them have
110 That mercy which true prayer ought to have.
  Bolingbroke Good aunt, stand up.
  Duchess.   Nay, do not say 'stand up';
Say 'pardon' first, and afterwards 'stand up'.

An if I were thy nurse, thy tongue to teach,
'Pardon' should be the first word of thy speech:
I never longed to hear a word till now,
Say 'pardon', king, let pity teach thee how.
The word is short, but not so short as sweet,
No word like 'pardon' for kings' mouths so meet.
　York. Speak it in French, king, say 'pardonne moy'.
　Duchess. Dost thou teach pardon pardon to destroy?　120
Ah, my sour husband, my hard-hearted lord,
That sets the word itself against the word!
Speak 'pardon' as 'tis current in our land—
The chopping French we do not understand.
Thine eye begins to speak, set thy tongue there:
Or in thy piteous heart plant thou thine ear,
That hearing how our plaints and prayers do pierce,
Pity may move thee 'pardon' to rehearse.
　Bolingbroke. Good aunt, stand up.
　Duchess.　　　　　　　　I do not sue to stand.
Pardon is all the suit I have in hand.　　　　　　130
　Bolingbroke. I pardon him, as God shall pardon me.
　Duchess. O happy vantage of a kneeling knee!
Yet am I sick for fear, speak it again,
Twice saying 'pardon' doth not pardon twain,
But makes one pardon strong.
　Bolingbroke.　　　　　　With all my heart
I pardon him.
　Duchess.　　A god on earth thou art.
　Bolingbroke. But for our trusty brother-in-law, and
　　　the abbot,
With all the rest of that consorted crew,
Destruction straight shall dog them at the heels.
Good uncle, help to order several powers　　　140
To Oxford, or where'er these traitors are.
They shall not live within this world, I swear,

But I will have them, if I once know where....
Uncle, farewell, and cousin too, adieu—
Your mother well hath prayed, and prove you true!
  Duchess. Come, my old son—I pray God make
    thee new.   [*they go*

[5. 4.]   SIR PIERCE OF EXTON *enters*
                 with his manservant

  Exton. Didst thou not mark the king, what words
    he spake?
'Have I no friend will rid me of this living fear?'
Was it not so?
  Servant.   These were his very words.
  Exton. 'Have I no friend?' quoth he—he spake
    it twice,
And urged it twice together, did he not?
  Servant. He did.
  Exton. And, speaking it, he wishtly looked on me,
As who should say, 'I would thou wert the man
That would divorce this terror from my heart',
10 Meaning the king at Pomfret....Come, let's go,
I am the king's friend, and will rid his foe.   [*they go*

[5. 5.]   *Pomfret Castle*

            '*RICHARD alone*'

  Richard. I have been studying how I may compare
This prison where I live unto the world:
And for because the world is populous,
And here is not a creature but myself,
I cannot do it; yet I'll hammer it out.

My brain I'll prove the female to my soul,
My soul the father, and these two beget
A generation of still-breeding thoughts:
And these same thoughts people this little world,
In humours like the people of this world: 10
For no thought is contented: the better sort,
As thoughts of things divine, are intermixed
With scruples, and do set the word itself
Against the word,
As thus: 'Come, little ones', and then again,
'It is as hard to come, as for a camel
To thread the postern of a small needle's eye'...
Thoughts tending to ambition, they do plot
Unlikely wonders: how these vain weak nails
May tear a passage through the flinty ribs   20
Of this hard world, my ragged prison walls;
And, for they cannot, die in their own pride.
Thoughts tending to content flatter themselves
That they are not the first of fortune's slaves,
Nor shall not be the last—like silly beggars
Who sitting in the stocks refuge their shame,
That many have and others must sit there:
And in this thought they find a kind of ease,
Bearing their own misfortunes on the back
Of such as have before endured the like....   30
Thus play I in one person many people,
And none contented: sometimes am I king,
Then treasons make me wish myself a beggar,
And so I am: then crushing penury
Persuades me I was better when a king;
Then am I kinged again, and by and by
Think that I am unkinged by Bolingbroke,
And straight am nothing....But whate'er I be,
Nor I, nor any man that but man is,

40 With nothing shall be pleased, till he be eased
  With being nothing....Music do I hear? [' *music plays* '
  Ha, ha! keep time—how sour sweet music is,
  When time is broke and no proportion kept!
  So is it in the music of men's lives:
  And here have I the daintiness of ear
  To check time broke in a disordered string;
  But for the concord of my state and time
  Had not an ear to hear my true time broke.
  I wasted time, and now doth time waste me:
50 For now hath time made me his numb'ring clock;
  My thoughts are minutes, and with sighs they jar
  Their watches on unto mine eyes, the outward watch,
  Whereto my finger, like a dial's point,
  Is pointing still, in cleansing them from tears.
  Now, sir, the sound that tells what hour it is
  Are clamorous groans which strike upon my heart,
  Which is the bell—so sighs, and tears, and groans,
  Show minutes, times, and hours: but my time
  Runs posting on in Bolingbroke's proud joy,
60 While I stand fooling here, his Jack of the clock....
  This music mads me, let it sound no more,
  For though it have holp madmen to their wits,
  In me it seems it will make wise men mad:
  Yet blessing on his heart that gives it me!
  For 'tis a sign of love; and love to Richard
  Is a strange brooch in this all-hating world.

'*Enter a Groom of the stable*'

  Groom. Hail, royal prince!
  Richard.   Thanks, noble peer;
  The cheapest of us is ten groats too dear.
  What art thou? and how comest thou hither,
70 Where no man never comes, but that sad dog

That brings me food to make misfortune live?
Groom. I was a poor groom of thy stable, king,
When thou wert king; who, travelling towards York,
With much ado at length have gotten leave
To look upon my sometimes royal master's face:
O, how it erned my heart when I beheld,
In London streets that coronation day,
When Bolingbroke rode on roan Barbary!
That horse that thou so often hast bestrid,
That horse that I so carefully have dressed!   80
Richard. Rode he on Barbary? tell me, gentle friend,
How went he under him?
Groom. So proudly as if he disdained the ground.
Richard. So proud that Bolingbroke was on his back...
That jade hath eat bread from my royal hand,
This hand hath made him proud with clapping him:
Would he not stumble? would he not fall down,
Since pride must have a fall, and break the neck
Of that proud man that did usurp his back?
Forgiveness, horse! why do I rail on thee,   90
Since thou, created to be awed by man,
Wast born to bear? I was not made a horse,
And yet I bear a burthen like an ass,
Spurred, galled, and tired by jaucing Bolingbroke.

'Enter one to Richard with meat'

Keeper. [*to the Groom*] Fellow, give place, here is no
      longer stay.
Richard. If thou love me, 'tis time thou wert away.
Groom. What my tongue dares not, that my heart
      shall say.   [*he goes*
Keeper. [*placing the dish upon the table*] My lord,
      will't please you to fall to?
Richard. Taste of it first, as thou art wont to do.

100   *Keeper.* My lord, I dare not, Sir Pierce of Exton, who
lately came from the king, commands the contrary.
 Richard. The devil take Henry of Lancaster and thee!
Patience is stale, and I am weary of it.
[he beats the Keeper
 Keeper. Help, help, help!

  EXTON *and the other murderers rush in*

 Richard. How now! what means death in this
  rude assault?
Villain, thy own hand yields thy death's instrument....
[he snatches an axe from one and kills him
Go thou, and fill another room in hell.
[he kills another, but 'here Exton strikes him down'
That hand shall burn in never-quenching fire
That staggers thus my person: Exton, thy fierce hand
110 Hath with the king's blood stained the king's own land....
Mount, mount, my soul! thy seat is up on high,
Whilst my gross flesh sinks downward, here to die.
[he dies
 Exton. As full of valour as of royal blood:
Both have I spilled. O, would the deed were good!
For now the devil that told me I did well
Says that this deed is chronicled in hell:
This dead king to the living king I'll bear....
Take hence the rest, and give them burial here.
[they carry out the bodies

[5. 6.]   *Windsor Castle*

  BOLINGBROKE *and the* DUKE OF YORK

 Bolingbroke. Kind uncle York, the latest news we hear,
Is that the rebels have consumed with fire

Our town of Cicester in Gloucestershire,
But whether they be ta'en or slain we hear not.

NORTHUMBERLAND enters

Welcome, my lord, what is the news?
  Northumberland. First, to thy sacred state wish I
    all happiness.
The next news is, I have to London sent
The heads of Salisbury, Spencer, Blunt and Kent.
The manner of their taking may appear
At large discoursèd in this paper here.   [*he presents it* 10
  Bolingbroke. We thank thee, gentle Percy, for
    thy pains,
And to thy worth will add right worthy gains.

FITZWATER enters

  Fitzwater. My lord, I have from Oxford sent
    to London
The heads of Brocas and Sir Bennet Seely,
Two of the dangerous consorted traitors,
That sought at Oxford thy dire overthrow.
  Bolingbroke. Thy pains, Fitzwater, shall not be forgot,
Right noble is thy merit, well I wot.

PERCY enters, with the BISHOP OF CARLISLE guarded

  Percy. The grand conspirator, Abbot of Westminster,
With clog of conscience and sour melancholy   20
Hath yielded up his body to the grave.
But here is Carlisle living, to abide
Thy kingly doom and sentence of his pride.
  Bolingbroke. Carlisle, this is your doom:
Choose out some secret place, some reverend room,
More than thou hast, and with it joy thy life;
So as thou liv'st in peace, die free from strife,

For though mine enemy thou hast ever been,
High sparks of honour in thee have I seen.

Enter EXTON, with persons bearing a coffin

30 *Exton.* Great king, within this coffin I present
Thy buried fear: herein all breathless lies
The mightiest of thy greatest enemies,
Richard of Bordeaux, by me hither brought.
 Bolingbroke. Exton, I thank thee not, for thou
  hast wrought
A deed of slander with thy fatal hand
Upon my head and all this famous land.
 Exton. From your own mouth, my lord, did I
  this deed.
 Bolingbroke. They love not poison that do poison need,
Nor do I thee; though I did wish him dead,
40 I hate the murderer, love him murderéd:
The guilt of conscience take thou for thy labour,
But neither my good word, nor princely favour:
With Cain go wander through the shades of night,
And never show thy head by day nor light....
Lords, I protest, my soul is full of woe,
That blood should sprinkle me to make me grow:
Come, mourn with me for what I do lament,
And put on sullen black incontinent.
I'll make a voyage to the Holy Land,
50 To wash this blood off from my guilty hand:
March sadly after, grace my mournings here,
In weeping after this untimely bier.
    [The coffin is borne slowly out, Bolingbroke
        and the rest following

GLOSSARY

Note. Where a pun or quibble is intended, the meanings are distinguished as (*a*) and (*b*)

ABIDE, endure; 5. 6. 22

ABSENT (adj.), 'absent time' = time of (the King's) absence (cf. *Oth.* 3. 4. 174); 2. 3. 79

ABUSE, ill-use, wrong; 2. 3. 137

ACCOMPLISHED, furnished, endowed, fully equipped (cf. *M.V.* 3. 4. 61); 2. 1. 177

ADVICE, deliberation, consultation; 1. 3. 233

ADVISED, deliberate, intentional; 1. 3. 188

AFFECT (sb.), kind feeling, affection (cf. *L.L.L.* 1. 1. 152, the only other instance in Sh.); 1. 4. 30

AFORE, before; 2. 1. 200

AGAINST, in anticipation of; 3. 4. 28

AMAZED, bewildered, distraught; 5. 2. 85; 5. 3. 22 (S.D.)

AMAZING, stupefying, confounding (cf. *M.N.D.* 4. 1. 145); 1. 3. 81

ANCIENT, (i) long-established; 1. 1. 9; (ii) former; 2. 1. 248

ANSWER, pay for, give account of; 1. 1. 38, 80, 198

ANTIC (sb.), (*a*) clown, mountebank, one who plays a grotesque or ludicrous part, (*b*) grinning face, gargoyle or death's head; 3. 2. 162

APISH, (*a*) imitative, (*b*) brutish; 2. 1. 22

APPARENT (cf. Lat. 'apparens'), plain, manifest; 1. 1. 13; 4. 1. 124

APPEACH, accuse, lay information against; 5. 2. 79, 102

APPEAL (sb.), impeachment of treason, accusation which the accuser is prepared to prove by combat; 1. 1. 4; 4. 1. 45, 79

APPEAL (vb.), accuse of a crime which the accuser undertakes to prove, esp. impeach of treason; 1. 1. 9, 27, 142

APPELLANT (adj.), appealing, accusing; 1. 1. 34

APPELLANT (sb.), one who appeals another, the challenger; 1. 3. 4; 4. 1. 104

APPOINTMENT, equipment (cf. *K. John,* 2. 1. 296); 3. 3. 53

APPREHENSION, thinking, conception; 1. 3. 300

APPROVE, prove, test; 1. 3. 112; 2. 3. 44

APRICOCK, apricot; 3. 4. 29

ARBITRATE, decide; 1. 1. 50, 200

ARGUMENT, subject, theme (cf. *1 Hen. IV,* 2. 4. 310); 1. 1. 12

AT ALL POINTS, completely; 1. 3. 2

ATONE, reconcile; 1. 1. 202

ATTACH, arrest; 2. 3. 156

ATTAINDER, foul or dishonouring accusation (cf. *L.L.L.* 1. 1. 157); 4. 1. 24

ATTEND, await; 1. 3. 116

ATTORNEY-GENERAL, a legal representative acting under a general power of attorney and representing his principal in all legal matters (*O.E.D.*); 2. 1. 203

AWE (sb.), power to inspire fear or reverence (cf. *J.C.* 2. 1. 52); 1. 1. 118

AWFUL, reverential; 3. 3. 76

AWRY, (*a*) obliquely, (*b*) wrongly; 2. 2. 19

BAFFLE, subject to public disgrace or infamy, treat with indignity (cf. *T.N.* 5. 1. 369 and 1 *Hen. IV*, 2. 4. 480 'hang me up by the heels' etc.). Orig. to hang up a recreant knight by the heels (cf. *F. Queene*, VI. vii. 27 'He by the heeles him hung vpon a tree, And baffuld so, that all which passed by, The picture of his punishment might see'); 1. 1. 170

BAIT (vb.), persecute, worry (as a dog worries an animal); 4. 1. 238

BALM, consecrated oil used in the coronation of a king; 3. 2. 55; 4. 1. 207

BAND, bond; 1. 1. 2; 2. 2. 71

BARBED, armed or caparisoned with a 'barb' or 'bard,' i.e. a covering for the breast and flanks of a war-horse, made of metal plates or of leather set with metal spikes or bosses; 3. 3. 117

BARREN, unresponsive, stupid (cf. *M.N.D.* 3. 2. 13; *Ham.* 3. 2. 46 'barren spectators'); 1. 3. 168

BASE COURT, the lower or outer courtyard of a castle (with a quibble on 'base,' despicable); 3. 3. 176, 180

BAY (sb.), a hunting term, lit. the chorus of barking raised by hounds in conflict with an animal, hence the animal's last stand; 2. 3. 128

BEADSMAN, almsman or pensioner (so called, because charged with the duty of offering prayers or 'beads' for his benefactor); 3. 2. 116

BENEVOLENCE, a forced loan levied without legal authority by the king, and first so called in 1473 by Edw. IV who exacted it as a token of goodwill (*O.E.D.*); 2. 1. 250

BETID, happened; 5. 1. 42

BETIMES, soon; 2. 1. 36

BIAS, a term at bowls, signifying the construction of the bowl to impart an oblique motion, or the oblique line in which it runs; 3. 4. 5.

BILL, a weapon consisting of a long staff with a curved blade at the end; 3. 2. 118

BLANK (sb.), a document with spaces left blank to be filled up at the pleasure of the person to whom it is granted, e.g. a blank charter; 2. 1. 250

BLAZE (sb.), flash, violent outburst (cf. *Ham.* 1. 3. 117); 2. 1. 33

BLEED, let blood; 1. 1. 157

BLEMISHED, stained; 2. 1. 293

BOISTEROUS, rough and violent; 1. 1. 4

BOOT, there is no boot = there is no help for it, no alternative; 1. 1. 164; it boots not = it avails not; 1. 3. 174; 3. 4. 18

BOUND (vb.), (i) limit, confine; 5. 2. 38; (ii) recoil, rebound; 1. 2. 58

BOY, knave, varlet. A term of abuse or contempt (cf. *Cor.* 5. 6. 113 and v. *Shrew*, G.); 4. 1. 65; (poss.) 5. 2. 69

BRAVING, defiant; 2. 3. 112, 143

BREATH, breathing-space, interval (cf. *Ric. III*, 4. 2. 24 'some breath, some little pause'); 3. 2. 164

BREED, brood, family, race; 2. 1. 45

BRING, accompany; 1. 3. 304

BROKEN, financially ruined; 2. 1. 257

BROKING, characterized by fraudulent dealing; 2. 1. 293

BROOK (vb.), endure, with some of the original meaning 'enjoy'; 3. 2. 2.

BUSINESS, anxiety, disturbance, serious purpose (cf. *O.E.D.*); 2. 2. 75

BUZZ, whisper busily (*O.E.D.* quotes Stubbes, *Anat. of Abuses*, 36 (1877) 'Hauing buzzed his venemous suggestions into their eares'); 2. 1. 26

BY, on account of; 2. 1. 52

CAITIFF, basely wretched; 1. 2. 53

CAREER, charge, encounter at a tournament or in battle; 1. 2. 49

CAREFUL, full of care, anxious; 2. 2. 75

CATERPILLAR, rapacious person, extortioner (cf. Gosson, 1579, *The Shoole of Abuse, Conteining a plesaunt inuectiue against . . . and such like Caterpillers of a Cõmonwelth*); 2. 3. 166

CHANGE (vb.), exchange; 3. 2. 189

CHECK (vb.), rebuke; 5. 5. 46

CHIVALRY, prowess; 1. 1. 203

CHOLER, (a) anger, (b) biliousness (cf. *Ham.* 3. 2. 306 and note); 1. 1. 153

CHOPPING, that changes the meaning (still in use in the prov. phrase 'chopping and changing'); 5. 3. 124

CLEAN, completely; 3. 1. 10

CLIMATE, region, country; 4. 1. 130

CLOG, impediment, burden, lit. a block of wood tied to the leg of an animal or prisoner to prevent escape; 5. 6. 20

CLOSE (sb.), the conclusion of a musical phrase, theme or movement, a cadence (cf. *Hen. V*, 1. 2. 182–3; *Tw. Nt.* 1. 1. 4); 2. 1. 12

COAT, coat of arms; 3. 1. 24

COMMENDS (sb.), greetings, compliments; 3. 3. 126

COMPARE BETWEEN, draw a comparison (*O.E.D.* gives no other examples); 2. 1. 185

COMPASSIONATE, displaying sorrowful emotion, (or) moving pity (*O.E.D.*). Not found elsewhere in latter sense before 1630. The context (esp. 'plaining') suggests that 'appealing for pity' is the meaning in Sh.'s mind; 1. 3. 174

COMPLAIN, bewail; 3. 4. 18

COMPLAIN ONESELF, bewail oneself, utter one's lamentations (cf. *Lucr.* 598); 1. 2. 42

COMPLOTTED, conspired; 1. 1. 96; 1. 3. 189

COMPOSITION, bodily structure or condition (cf. *K. John*, 1. 1. 88); 2. 1. 73

CONCEIT, fancy, fantasy; 2. 2. 33

CONCLUDE, come to final terms; 1. 1. 156

CONDITION, (*a*) personal quality (cf. *L.L.L.* 5. 2. 20); 2. 3. 107; (*b*) condition, circumstances; 2. 3. 108

CONFINE (sb.), territory; 3. 2. 125

CONFOUND, destroy; 3. 4. 60; 4. 1. 141; 5. 3. 86

CONJURATION, appeal, 'senseless conjuration' = appeal to inanimate things; 3. 2. 23

CONSENT TO, be accomplice in; 1. 2. 25

CONSORTED, associated, leagued (cf. *L.L.L.* 1. 1. 253); 5. 3. 138; 5. 6. 15

CONTRIVE, plot, scheme; 1. 1. 96

CONVERT (vb. intr.), change, undergo a change (cf. *Mach.* 4. 3. 229); 5. 1. 66; 5. 3. 64

CONVEYER, (*a*) one that transports or transfers, (*b*) a thief; (v. note) 4. 1. 317

COUSIN, kinsman; 2. 1. 109; 2. 2. 118

CRAFT, (*a*) guile, deceit, (*b*) a manual art; 1. 4. 28

CROSSLY, athwart, adversely; 2. 4. 24

CROWN (sb.), (*a*) the King's crown, (*b*) head; 3. 3. 95, 96

CUNNING, skilfully contrived, that which requires skill (to play); 1. 3. 163

CURRENT, valid, having currency (like coin); 1. 3. 231

DATE (sb.), period; 5. 2. 91

DATELESS, limitless, eternal; 1. 3. 151

DEAD, pale as death (cf. *2 Hen. IV*, 1. 1. 71 'so dead in look'); 3. 2. 79

DEAR, (i) of great value; 2. 1. 57–8, (ii) dire, grievous; 1. 3. 151; (iii) 'a dear account' comprises both meanings; 1. 1. 130

DECEIVABLE, deceitful, deceptive; 2. 3. 84

DEFEND, forbid; 1. 3. 18

DEGREE, (i) manner; 2. 3. 109; (ii) one 'step' in direct descent; 1. 4. 36; (iii) 'in any fair degree' = to any reasonable extent according to the code of chivalry; 1. 1. 80

DEPOSE, examine on oath; 1. 3. 30

DEPRESS, bring low, humble; 3. 4. 68

DESIGN (sb.), project, enterprise; 1. 1. 81; 1. 3. 45

DESIGN (vb.), indicate, designate; 1. 1. 203

DESPISED, despicable; 2. 3. 95

DETERMINATE, a legal term = set a limit to, terminate (cf. *Son.* 87. 4 'My bonds in thee are all determinate'); 1. 3. 150

DETESTED, detestable; 2. 3. 109; 3. 2. 44

DIGRESSING, transgressing (cf. *Tit.* 5. 3. 116); 5. 3. 66

DISCOMFORTABLE, destroying comfort or happiness; 3. 2. 36

DISPARK, convert land where game is preserved to other uses; 3. 1. 23

DISTAFF-WOMAN, spinning-woman; 3. 2. 118

DIVINE, immortal (cf. *Lucr.* 1164); 1. 1. 38

DOUBT ('TIS), 'tis feared; 3. 4. 69

DUTY, homage, an expression of submission, deference or respect; 3. 3. 48, 188

EAGER, sharp (cf. *Ham.* 1. 4. 2); 1. 1. 49

EAR (vb.), plough, till; 3. 2. 212

EARTH, country, land, domain; 2. 1. 41, 50

EFFEMINATE, self-indulgent, voluptuous; 5. 3. 10

ENDOWMENT, property from which one derives income; 2. 3. 139

ENFRANCHISEMENT, (i) liberation; 1. 3. 90; (ii) admission (here restoration) to political rights; 3. 3. 114

ENSUE, follow, succeed, approach (cf. *Lucr.* 502, *Ric. III*, 2. 3. 43); 'Used of something about to happen, not necessarily regarded as a consequence' (Gordon); 2. 1. 68, 197

ENTREAT, treat; 3. 1. 37

ENVY (sb.), malice, enmity; 2. 1. 49

ERNE, grieve. Mod. edd. follow F. and print 'yearn' (= desire) with which it was often confused in Eliz. Eng. (cf. *M.W.W.* 3. 5. 45); 5. 5. 76

EVENT, outcome, consequence; 2. 1. 214

EXACTLY, in express terms, precisely (*O.E.D.* quotes from 1646); 1. 1. 140

EXCEPT (vb.), take exception to (*O.E.D.* but cf. *O.E.D.* 3, allege as an objection); 1. 1. 72

EXCLAIM (sb.), exclamation, outcry; 1. 2. 2

EXPEDIENCE, speed; 2. 1. 287

EXPEDIENT, speedy (cf. *John*, 2. 1. 60); 1. 4. 39

EXTINCT, extinguished, quenched; 1. 3. 222

EXTREMITY, IN, to the utmost (cf. *M.N.D.* 3. 2. 3); 2. 2. 72

FACE, (*a*) brazen out, (*b*) adorn; lit. 'trim'; 4. 1. 285

FAINT (vb. and adj.), (be) faint-hearted; 2. 1. 297; 2. 2. 32

FALL (vb.), let fall, drop; 3. 4. 104

FANTASTIC, existing only in imagination; 1. 3. 299

FARM (sb.), the letting out of public revenue for a fixed payment; 2. 1. 60 (with a quibble on 'farm' = farmstead), 256

FARM (vb.), lease the right of taxing to the highest bidder, on consideration of a fixed cash payment; 1. 4. 45

FAVOUR (sb.), (*a*) countenance, (*b*) good-will; 4. 1. 168

FEARFUL, timorous; 3. 3. 73

FEMALE, small and weak, like a woman's; 3. 2. 114

FETCH, derive, draw as from a source; 1. 1. 97

FIGURE, image; 4. 1. 125

FLATTER, (i) try to please by obsequious speech; 2. 1. 87, 90; (ii) inspire with hope on insufficient grounds (*O.E.D.* quotes Fleming cont. Holinshed iii. 1351/1 'My lord, you are verie sicke, I will not flatter with you'); 2. 1. 89

FLATTER WITH, fawn upon (cf. *Tw. Nt.* 1. 5. 307); 2. 1. 88

FOIL (sb.), (*a*) defeat (orig. a term in wrestling), (*b*) that which sets off something to advantage; 1. 3. 266

FOND, foolish; 5. 2. 95, 101; 5. 1. 101 (with a quibble on 'tender')

FONDLY, (i) tenderly; 3. 2. 9; (ii) foolishly; 3. 3. 185; 4. 1. 72

FOR ME, for my part; 1. 4. 6

FOR WHY, because; 5. 1. 46

FRANTIC, lunatic, mad; 3. 3. 185

FREE, without constraint; 1. 3. 115

FRET (vb.), form by wearing away; 3. 3. 167

GAGE (sb.), pledge, usually a glove or gauntlet; 1. 1. 69, 146; 4. 1. 25 *etc.*; 'in gage,' in pledge; 4. 1. 34

GLASS, lens of the eye (cf. *Wint.* 1. 2. 268 'eye-glass'; *Cor.* 3. 2. 117 'the glasses of my sight'); 1. 3. 208

GLISTERING, glittering; 3. 3. 178

GLOSE, talk smoothly and speciously, flatter; 2. 1. 10

GNARL, snarl (cf. 2 *Hen. VI*, 3. 1. 192 'And wolves are gnarling who shall gnaw thee'—the only other instance in Sh.); 1. 3. 292

GOLGOTHA, graveyard, charnel-house; 4. 1. 144

GRIEF, hardship, suffering; 1. 3. 258

GRIPE, seize, grasp tightly (cf. 1 *Hen. IV*, 5. 1. 57); 2. 1. 189

HAPPILY, (either) haply (or) happily. The two forms are both found in Sh. and were practically interchangeable; 5. 3. 22

HAPPY, well-endowed; 3. 1. 9

HARDLY, with difficulty; 2. 4. 2

HATEFUL, full of hatred; 2. 2. 140

HAUGHT, haughty; 4. 1. 254

HAVIOUR, bearing, carriage; 1. 3. 77

HEIGHT, high rank; 1. 1. 189

HEIR, offspring; 2. 2. 63

HIGH-STOMACHED, haughty (cf. *Ps.* ci. 7, Prayer-book ver. 'a proud look and high stomach'); 1. 1. 18

HUMOUR, whim; 5. 5. 10

IMP (vb.), a term of falconry, meaning to engraft feathers in the wing of a bird to restore or improve its powers of flight; hence, enlarge, extend, eke; 2. 1. 292

IMPEACH, discredit, disparage (cf. *M.N.D.* 2. 1. 214); 1. 1. 170, 189

IMPRESE, for Ital. 'impresa,' a heraldic device, impressed, engraved or painted upon a shield with an attached motto or 'word'; much affected by noblemen of fashion at this time; 3. 1. 25

INCONTINENT (adv.), straightway, at once; 5. 6. 48

INDIFFERENT, impartial; 2. 3. 116

INFECTION, evil or corrupting influence, contamination, moral or physical (v. *O.E.D.* 6 and 7); 2. 1. 44

INHABITABLE, uninhabitable (cf. Jonson, *Catiline*, 5. 1. 54 'some inhabitable place'); 1. 1. 65

IN HASTE WHEREOF, to hasten which; 1. 1. 150

INHERIT, (i) *trans.* put in possession, lit. make heir; the only instance of this use in Sh.; 1. 1. 85; (ii) *intrans.* hold, possess; 2. 1. 83

INJURIOUS, wilfully inflicting injury, 'almost = insolent' (Gordon); 1. 1. 91

INTERCHANGEABLY, mutually, reciprocally; 1. 1. 146; 5. 2. 98

JACK OF THE CLOCK, an automatic figure which strikes the quarters, etc., on a bell; 5. 5. 60

JADE, vicious or unreliable horse; 5. 5. 85

JAR (vb.), tick; 5. 5. 51

JAUNCING, prancing (*O.E.D.* with a query; cf. Q2 *Rom.* 2. 5. 53); 5. 5. 94

JEST (vb.), to play a part in a pageant, masque, masquerade or the like (v. note); 1. 3. 95

JOURNEYMAN, (*a*) traveller, (*b*) one who works under a master-craftsman for day wages; 1. 3. 274

JOY, enjoy; 5. 6. 26

KERN (derived from Irish 'ceithern' = a band of footsoldiers), a light-armed Irish foot-soldier; 2. 1. 156

KNOT (sb.), a flower-bed or garden laid out in an intricate design; 3. 4. 46

LARGE (AT), in full; 3. 1. 41; 5. 6. 10

LARGESS, lavish expenditure in gifts; 1. 4. 44

LAST, lately, recently; 1. 1. 131

LEARN, teach; 4. 1. 120

LENDINGS, 'money advanced to soldiers when the regular pay cannot be given' (*O.E.D.*); 1. 1. 89

LETTERS-PATENT, an open letter from a sovereign conferring some right, privilege, title, property or office; 2. 1. 202; 2. 3. 130

LEWD, base; 1. 1. 90

LIBERAL, free; 2. 1. 229

LINEAL, transmitted by lineal descent; 3. 3. 113

LINGER, prolong (cf. *M.N.D.* 1. 1. 4 'lingers my desires,' *Oth.* 4. 2. 231); 2. 2. 72

LINING, contents (cf. *A.Y.L.* 2. 7. 154 'belly with good capon lined'); 1. 4. 61

LODGE, throw down on the ground, beat down (cf. *Macb.* 4. 1. 55); 3. 3. 162

LOOK UPON, look on, as a mere spectator (cf. *3 Hen. VI*, 2. 3. 27); 4. 1. 237

LOOK WHEN, expect that; 1. 3. 243

MAIM (sb.), mutilation or loss of some essential part, serious injury (cf. *1 Hen. IV*, 4. 1. 42); 1. 3. 156

MAKE, do; 5. 3. 89

MANAGE (sb.), (i) management, conduct of affairs (cf. *M.V.* 3. 4. 25 and *John*, 1. 1. 37); 1. 4. 39; (ii) the directing of a horse in its paces; 3. 3. 179

MANAGE (vb.), wield; 3. 2. 118

MANNER (IN), so to speak, as it were; 3. 1. 11

MANUAL SEAL, authorized warrant, lit. document sealed by the hand of the competent authority; 4. 1. 25

MAP, epitome, embodiment; 5. 1. 12

MEAN (adj.), poor, humble; 1. 2. 33

MEASURE (sb.), (i) a stately dance; 1. 3. 291; (ii) (a) a dance, (b) moderation, temperance; 3. 4. 7, 8

MEASURE (vb.), traverse; 3. 2. 125

MERELY, purely; 2. 1. 243

MERIT, due reward; 1. 3. 156

METTLE, essence, stuff (cf. Ric. III, 4. 4. 302 'Even of your mettle, of your very blood'); 1. 2. 23

MODEL (sb.), (i) copy; 1. 2. 28; (ii) representation or facsimile on a small scale; 3. 2. 153; 3. 4. 42; (iii) ground plan; 5. 1. 11

MOE, more; 2. 1. 239

MORTAL, deadly; 3. 2. 21

MOTIVE, moving organ, instrument (cf. Troil. 4. 5. 57); 1. 1. 193

NATIVE, by right of birth (cf. 3 Hen. VI, 3. 3. 190 'native right'); 3. 2. 25

NEAR, nearer; 3. 2. 64; 5. 1 88.

NICELY, (a) subtly, (b) triflingly (cf. Rom. 5. 2. 18; Caes. 4. 3. 8); 2. 1. 84

NOBLE = 20 groats or 6s. 8d.; 1. 1. 88

NOTE, stigma, mark of disgrace. From Lat. 'nota' = 'the technical term for the official and public reprehensions of private persons by the Censor' (Herford) (cf. Lucr. 208, L.L.L. 4. 3. 122); 1. 1. 43

NOTHING LESS, anything but. Obsolete idiom; cf. Fr. rien moins que (O.E.D. 'less' B. 3); 2. 2. 34

NUMBERING, which counts the hours; 5. 5. 50

OBJECT (vb.), bring as a charge; 1. 1. 28

OBSCENE, repulsive, foul; 4. 1. 131

OFFICE, service; 2. 2. 139

ORDER, direct, regulate; 5. 3. 140

OSTENTATION, display; 2. 3. 95

OUT-DARED, dared down, cowed (Herford); 1. 1. 190

OVER-PROUD, too luxuriant. 'Proud' and 'pride' often denote hot-bloodedness in men and animals (cf. L.L.L. 5. 2. 66, Lucr. 712, Two Gent. G. and Errors G.); 3. 4. 59

OWE, own, possess; 4. 1. 185

PAIN OF LIFE (ON), on pain of death. The expression 'on pain of,' now 'followed by the penalty or punishment incurred,' was also formerly followed by 'that which one is liable to pay or forfeit' (O.E.D. 'pain' 1 b); 1. 3. 140 (v. note), 153

PALE (sb.), fence, enclosure; 3. 4. 40

PARLE, a meeting to discuss terms under a truce, a trumpet-call to such a meeting; 1. 1. 192; 3. 3. 33

PARTIAL SLANDER, accusation of being partial; 1. 3. 241

PARTIALIZE, render partial or one-sided; 1. 1. 120

PARTY, part, side; 3. 3. 115

PARTY-VERDICT, one share in a joint verdict; 1. 3. 234

PASSAGE, wandering, travel; 1. 3. 272

PASSENGER, passer-by; 5. 3. 9

PAWN (sb.), pledge or gage of battle; 1. 1. 74

PEACEFUL, unopposed; 3.2.125

PELICAN. The female bird is said to feed or revive her young with her blood (cf. *Ham.* 4. 5. 146) but here Shakespeare puts the initiative on the young; 2. 1. 126

PELTING, paltry, petty; 2. 1. 60

PERSPECTIVE, (*a*) any sort of glass for aiding or distorting the sight; cf. *All's Well*, 5. 3. 48 'his scornful perspective ...Which warped the line of every other favour'; (*b*) 'a kind of relief in which the surface was so modelled as to produce, when seen from the side, the impression of a continuous picture, which, when seen from the front, disappeared' (Herford); 2. 2. 18

PHAETHON. The type of youthful presumption. The son of Helios, who, having obtained from his father permission to drive the sun's chariot for a day, lost control of the steeds, and was struck down by a thunderbolt of Jupiter, to prevent his setting the earth on fire; 3. 3. 178

PILL (vb.), plunder, despoil; 2. 1. 246

PINE (vb.), torment, afflict; 5. 1. 77

PITCH (sb.), the height to which a falcon rises; 1. 1. 109

PITY (vb. and sb.) (have) mercy, pardon; 5. 3. 57 (2)

PLAINING, lamentation, complaint; 1. 3. 175

PLATED, armed (cf. *Ant. & Cleo.* 1. 1. 4); 1. 3. 28

POMPOUS, magnificently apparelled, dressed for ceremony; 4. 1. 250

POSSESSED, (*a*) in possession of, (*b*) dominated by an evil spirit; 2. 1. 107–8

POST (adv.), at express speed; 5. 2. 112

POST (vb.), ride fast, hasten; 1. 1. 56

POSTERN, small back (or side) door; 5 5. 17

POWER, body of troops; 3. 2. 186,211; 5. 3.140; 2.2.126

PRECEDENT, instance proving a fact; 2. 1. 130

PRESENCE, reception-room, presence-chamber at court; 1. 3. 289

PRESENCE (IN), present; 4. 1.62

PRESENTLY, at once; 1. 4. 52; 2. 2. 92; 3. 2. 179

PRESS (vb.), force to serve in the army; 3. 2. 58

PRESS TO DEATH, kill by placing heavy weights on the chest (the punishment for a felon who refused to speak); 3. 4. 72

PREVENTION, baffling or stopping another person in the execution of his designs; 2. 1. 167

PRICK, urge, incite; 2. 1. 207;
2. 3. 78

PROCESS, onward movement in
space, progress; 2. 3. 12

PRODIGY, a monstrous or un-
natural birth; 2. 2. 64

PROFANE (vb.), (i) misuse (cf.
2 *Hen. IV*, 2. 4. 391); 1. 3.
59; (ii) commit sacrilege;
3. 3. 81

PROOF, invulnerability, lit.
strength tested or proved
(cf. mod. 'rain-proof'); fre-
quently used of armour (cf.
Ham. 2. 2. 494; 3. 4. 38);
1. 3. 73

PROPERTY, characteristic or
essential quality; 3. 2. 135

PROUD, v. *over-proud*; 3. 4. 59

PURCHASE, acquire; 1. 3. 282

PURGE, (*a*) purify the body of
disease or humours, by
bleeding or purgatives, (*b*)
a legal term = clear from
accusation of guilt; 1. 1. 153

QUIT, requite, repay; 5. 1. 43

RAGE (sb.), (i) (*a*) flood,
sudden rising of the sea,
(*b*) violent passion; 3. 2.
109; (ii) fury, violence;
3. 3. 59

RAGGED, rugged, rough, un-
tamed; 2. 1. 70 (v. note);
5. 5. 21

RANKLE, cause a festering
wound (cf. *Ric. III*, 1. 3.
291); 1. 3. 302

RAPIER, long pointed sword for
thrusting (superseded the
shorter 'broadsword' for
hacking, c. 1590); 4. 1. 40

RASH, operating quickly or
strongly (cf. 2 *Hen. IV*, 4. 4.
48); 2. 1. 33

RAVEL OUT, disentangle, make
clear (cf. *Hamlet* G.); 4. 1.
228

RAW, crude, unripe; 2. 3. 42

RAZE, obliterate; 3. 1. 25

READ A LECTURE, deliver a
lecture or sermon; 4. 1. 232

REBUKE, shame, disgrace; 2. 1.
166

RECEIPT, a sum of money received (not an acknow-
ledgment of receipt); 1. 1.
126

RECORD (sb.), witness; 1. 1. 30

RECREANT (sb. and adj.), one
who yields in combat, hence.
cowardly, craven; 1. 1.
144; 1. 2. 53; 1. 3. 106, 111

REFUGE (vb.), shelter, shield;
5. 5. 26

REGARD (sb.), thoughtful attention, consideration; 1. 3.
216; 2. 1. 28

REGREET, greet, salute; 1. 3.
67, 142, 186

REHEARSE, recite in a formal
manner; 5. 3. 128

REMEMBER, remind; 1. 3. 269

REPEAL (vb.), recall from exile;
2. 2. 49; 4. 1. 85

RESTFUL, peaceful; 4. 1. 12

RETIRE, withdraw, lead back;
2. 2. 46

RETURN, 'state by way of a report or verdict' (*O.E.D.* 16);
1. 3. 122

REVERSION (IN), a legal term:
lit. 'conditional upon the
expiry of a grant or the
death of a person' (*O.E.D.*)
but in Sh. generally = (i)
prospectively (cf. *Troil.* 3. 2.
100); 1. 4. 35; (ii) to be
realized in the future; 2. 2. 38

RID, make away with, kill
(cf. *Temp.* 1. 2. 364); 5. 4. 11

RIGHT (adv.), righteously; 1. 1. 46

RIGHT (sb.), that which justly accrues to anyone, what one may properly claim; 2. 1. 190, 201; 2. 3. 120

RIGHTLY, (a) directly, from in front, (b) properly; 2. 2. 18

ROUNDLY, (a) glibly (O.E.D. 6), (b) bluntly, unceremoniously (O.E.D. 3); 2. 1. 122

ROUSE, start an animal from its lair; 2. 3. 128

ROYALTY, royal prerogative or right granted by the sovereign to an individual; 2. 1. 190; 2. 3. 120; 3. 3. 113

RUB (sb.), a term at bowls meaning an impediment or obstacle; 3. 4. 4

RUE (vb.), repent; 1. 3. 205

RUG, lit. 'a sort of coarse frieze,' hence = shaggy material of any kind; 2. 1. 156

RUTH, pity; 3. 4. 106

SAFE, 'placed beyond the power of doing harm' (O.E.D. 10) (cf. Macb. 3. 4. 25); 5. 3. 41

SCOPE, (i) object, aim; 3. 3. 112; (ii) opportunity, 'room' to act; 3. 3. 140, 141

SCRUPLE, doubt; 5. 5. 13

SECURE, careless, over-confident; 5. 3. 43

SECURELY, without care or apprehension; 1. 3. 97; 2. 1. 266

SEE, see to, attend to (cf. Shrew, 1. 2. 145 and Ant. & Cleo. 5. 2. 368); 2. 1. 217

SEIZE, (i) take possession of; 2. 1. 160; (ii) (a) take hold of with the hands, (b) take forcible possession of; 4. 1. 181

SELF, same; 1. 2. 23

SELF-BORNE, borne for oneself, i.e. in civil war; 2. 3. 80 (v. note)

SENSELESS, v. conjuration; 3. 2. 23

SET (vb.), (i) hold, regard; 1. 3. 293; (ii) put up a stake, (here) challenge; 4. 1. 57

SEVERAL, distinct, various; 1. 3. 51; 5. 3. 140

SHADOW, delusive semblance or image (O.E.D. 6 a); 2. 2. 14

SHEER, clear, unpolluted; 5. 3. 61

SHREWD, hurtful, injurious; 3. 2. 59

SIFT, discover a man's 'true... designs by dexterous questioning' (Herford) (cf. Ham. 2. 2. 58); 1. 1. 12

SIGNORY, domain, estate; 3. 1. 22; 4. 1. 89

SILLY, simple; 5. 5. 25

SLY, stealthy; 1. 3. 150

SMALL AND SMALL (BY), little by little; 3. 2. 198

SOLICIT, petition, importune; 1. 2. 2

SOMETIME (adj.), former; 5. 1. 37

SOMETIME(s) (adv.), formerly; 4. 1. 169; 5. 5. 75

SOOTH, used as a sb. of 'soothe' = blandishment, flattery (cf. Per. 1. 2. 44 'Signior Sooth' and K. John, 3. 1. 121 'soothe up'); 3. 3. 136

SORT, set, crew, pack (cf. M.N.D. 3. 2. 13 'that barren sort' and Ric. III, 5. 3. 316); 4. 1. 246

Sour, bitter; 4. 1. 241

Sport (make), provide amusement, take pleasure; 2. 1. 85

Spot (sb. and vb.), disgrace, stain; 1. 1. 175; 3. 2. 134

Sprightfully, spiritedly, with great spirit; 1. 3. 3

Stagger, cause to reel; 5. 5. 109

Stand on, be contingent on; 4. 1. 33

Stand out, hold out; 1. 4. 38

Stand upon, be incumbent on (cf. *Ham.* 5. 2. 63); 2. 3. 138

Star, rank (v. *Ham.* G.); 4. 1. 21

State, (*a*) government, (*b*) majesty; 1. 3. 190; 3. 2. 72, 117, 163; 3. 4. 27; 4. 1. 179, 192, 209, 252; 5. 1. 18; 5. 5. 47; 5. 6. 6

Sterling (be), have value, be current; 4. 1. 264

Stop (the ear), render deaf to something (*O.E.D.* 8 *a*); 2. 1. 17

Stranger, alien, foreign; 1. 3. 143

Stream (vb.), cause to float in the wind; 4. 1. 94

Strike, (*a*) furl sails, (*b*) deal or aim a blow; 2. 1. 266

Subscribe, put one down for (a sum of money); 1. 4. 50

Substitute, deputy; 1. 4. 48

Sue livery, institute a suit for the delivery or surrender of lands which were in the hands of the feudal suzerain until the heir could prove he was of age; 2. 1. 203; 2. 3. 129

Suggest, prompt to evil, tempt; 1. 1. 101; 3. 4. 75

Sullen, melancholy. 'Sometimes with the notion of passing heavily, moving sluggishly' (*O.E.D.*); 1. 3. 227, 265; 5. 6. 48

Sullens, a morbid state of sullenness, sulks (cf. Dryden, *Troil. & Cress.* 4. 2 'I'll e'en go home, and shut up my doors, and die o' the sullens, like an old bird in a cage'); 2. 1. 139

Supplant, root out, 2. 1. 156

Sympathize, answer or correspond to; 5. 1. 46

Sympathy, consonance, equality (in rank); 4. 1. 33

Tap out, draw out (i.e. liquor from a cask); 2. 1. 127

Tardy, slow, making little progress; 2. 1. 22

Tear, wound, lacerate; 3. 3. 83

Teeming, fruitful, productive; 2. 1. 51; 5. 2. 91

Tender (vb.), (*a*) be concerned for or solicitous about, (*b*) offer, allege (cf. *Ham.* 1. 3. 107); 1. 1. 32

Tenement, land or real property held of another by any tenure; 2. 1. 60

Thought, melancholy consideration (cf. *Ham.* 3. 1. 85; 4. 5. 187 and G.); 2. 2. 31; 5. 5. 51

Thrive to, succeed in; 2. 2. 146

Throw, cast dice; 4. 1. 57

Tied, bound, obliged; 1. 1. 63

Time, (i) the life of a man (cf. *Ant. & Cleo.* 3. 2. 59 'the time'); 1. 1. 177; (ii) season; 1. 3. 220

Timeless, untimely; 4. 1. 5

Toiled, exhausted with toil; 4. 1. 96

Touch, fingering (of a musical instrument), note; 1. 3. 165

Trade (sb.), passage to and fro, resort; 3. 3. 156

Trespass (sb.), a violation of the law, properly one not amounting to treason or felony; 1. 1. 138; 5. 2. 89

Triumph (sb.), a public festivity, esp. a tournament; 5. 2. 52; 5. 3. 14

True, loyal; 2. 1. 192

Truth, loyalty (cf. *untruth*, 2. 2. 102 and 'truth' *K. John* G.); 5. 2. 44

Twain (vb.), divide, hence weaken; 5. 3. 134

Unavoided, unavoidable (cf. *Ric. III*, 4. 4. 217); 2. 1. 268

Uncivil, barbarous, uncivilized (cf. *F. Queene*, II. vii. 3 'An vncouth, saluage, and vnciuile wight'); 3. 3. 102

Undeaf, restore hearing to; 2. 1. 16

Underbearing, endurance; 1. 4. 29

Undo, (*a*) ruin, (*b*) undress; 4. 1. 203

Unfelt, intangible (cf. *Lucr.* 828), 'not accompanied by any palpable proofs'(Wright); 2. 3. 61

Ungracious, graceless, profane; 2. 3. 89

Unhappy (vb.), make unhappy or unfortunate; 3. 1. 10

Unpeopled, without servants (cf. *L.L.L.* 2. 1. 88, note). 'People' commonly = servants, retinue in Sh. (cf. *M.W.W.* 2. 2. 52, *Tw. Nt.* 1. 5. 112); 1. 2. 69

Unthrifty, profligate as well as prodigal; 5. 3. 1

Untruth, unfaithfulness, treason (cf. *truth*, 5. 2. 44 and 'truth' *K. John* G.); 2. 2. 102

Uplifted, taken up in defence; 2. 2. 50

Urge (vb.), insist on; 3. 1. 4; 4. 1. 271; 5. 4. 5

Vantage, profit; 5. 3. 132

Venom (adj.), venomous; 2. 1. 19

Venom (sb.), poison, esp. that secreted by snakes; 2. 1. 157

Verge, (*a*) rim or circle of metal (cf. *Ric. III*, 4. 1. 59 'The inclusiue Verge of Golden Mettall, that must round my Brow'), (*b*) 'the compass about the king's court, which extended for twelve miles round' (Clar.); 2. 1. 102

Wanton (adj.), (i) trifling, frivolous; 5. 1. 101; (ii) spoilt, pampered; 5. 3. 10

Wantons (play the), dally, trifle; 3. 3. 164

Warder, a staff or truncheon used to give the signal for the commencement or cessation of hostilities; 1. 3. 118

Waste, with a play on the legal term = 'destruction of houses, wood, or other produce of land, done by the tenant to the prejudice of the freehold' (Wright); 2. 1. 103

Watch (sb.), (i) 'the marks of the minutes on a dial-plate' (Schmidt); (ii) dial, clock-face; 5. 5. 52

Watching, sleeplessness (cf. *Ham.* 2. 2. 148); 2. 1. 78

WHERE, whereas; 3. 2. 185

WHILE, until (cf. *Macb.* 3. 1.
44); 1. 3. 122

WILL, inclination, desire; 2. 1.
28

WISHTLY, earnestly, intently
and longingly (v. *O.E.D.*
'wishly'); 5. 4. 7

WIT, sound sense or judgment;
2. 1. 28

WORTHY, merited (cf. *All's
Well*, 4 3. 7); 5. 1. 68

WRACK (sb.), (*a*) shipwreck,
(*b*) an instrument of tor-
ture; 2. 1. 267, 269

ZEAL, devotion, loyalty (often
'religious fervour,' cf. *K.
John*, 2. 1. 565); 1. 1. 47

WORDSWORTH CLASSICS

General Editors: Marcus Clapham and Clive Reynard
Other titles in this series

DISTRIBUTION

AUSTRALIA
Treasure Press
22 Salmon Street
Port Melbourne
Vic 3207
Tel: (03) 646 6716
Fax: (03) 646 6925

DENMARK
BOG-FAN
St. Kongensgade 61A
1264 København K

BOGPA SIKA
Industrivej 1
7120 Vejle Ø

FRANCE
Bookking International
16 Rue Des Grands Augustins
75006 Paris
France

GERMANY
Swan Buch-Marketing GmbH
Goldscheuerstrabe 16
D-7640 Kehl Am Rhein
Germany

GREAT BRITAIN
Wordsworth Editions Ltd
8B East Street
Ware
Herts SG12 9HU

Selecta Books
The Selectabook Distribution Centre
Folly Road, Roundway
Devizes
Wilts SN10 2HR

HOLLAND & BELGIUM
Uitgeverlj En Boekhandel
Van Gennep BV
Spuistraat 283
1012 VR Amsterdam
Holland

IRELAND
Wordsworth Editions Ltd
c/o Roberts Books
Unit 12
Benson Street
Enterprise Centre
Hanover Quay
Dublin 2

ITALY
Magis Books
Piazza Della Vittoria 1/C
42100 Reggio Emilia
Tel: 0522-452303
Fax: 0522-452845

NORWAY
Norsk Bokimport AS
Bertrand Narvesensvei 2
Postboks 6219
Etterstad
0602 Oslo
Norway

SOUTH AFRICA
Trade Winds Press (Pty) Ltd
P O Box 20194
Durban North 4016
South Africa

SWEDEN
Akademibokhandelsgruppen
Box 21002
100 31 Stockholm